SPIRITUAL SHOWDOWNS

SCRIPTURES OF SOUL

VOLUME 1

by

GRACIOUS GUIDE GUNJ

Clever Fox® PUBLISHING

Chennai • Bangalore

CLEVER FOX PUBLISHING
Chennai, India

Published by CLEVER FOX PUBLISHING 2026

ISBN: 978-93-7500-563-6

CONTENTS

A NOTE OF GRATITUDE

Before these pages begin to speak, I pause to bow.

To the unseen hands that have held me long before I learned how to hold myself.

I begin with gratitude to thank my Guru's…all who arrived in form and those who arrived as silence, circumstance, breakdown or sudden clarity. Some taught me through words, some through presence and some through pain. Each one carved a doorway in my awareness. Each one guided me closer to truth.

To, Maa Shakti…my fire, my endurance, my becoming, my soul.

To, Shiva…my guru, my stillness, my storm, my dissolver.

To, Hanuman ji…my strength, my protector.

To, Maha Avatar Babaji…my eternal witness, my guide.

To all the Divine Energies that moved through my life as strength when I felt weak, as guidance when I felt lost, as healing when I felt broken.

To my Guru, SarasMa..
your guidance, your love, your care, your relentless efforts
have carved the most important part of my life. You introduced me to my true strength and showed me how to stand back up and claim my life back.
I'm eternally grateful to you Ma.

To my mother, Minna
the true warrior of our family. Time and again, you pulled us out of the darkest moments, guided by a strength that came from

above and an awareness that always knew when to act. I honour you.

To my father, Amarjeet
for opening my world in the early 80's..through cinema, oriental cuisine, experiences that stayed. Your large-hearted spirit and tireless presence, driving us through life, even in your eighties papa, will live on in me.

To my Big Brother, Monit
my constant anchor, my unwavering support,
your strength, reliability and the generous way you've cared for our parents, holds a gratitude that only heavens can define.

I truly thank you for shaping my early life.
Not a simple one.. but a life that allowed me to live many lives within one body. For the challenges we faced together, for the lessons we survived together and for the foundation..visible and invisible..that made me who I am today.

To my daughter Sum, my firstborn.
I am deeply grateful for you..my saviour, my anchor, my awakener.
You have gently yet firmly pushed me beyond boundaries I once refused to leave.
May life bless you with all its richness and may you share your generosity to uplift others

To my son, Nam, my second born, you're wise
far beyond your years.
You came into my life with insight and intensity. I held both with love.
The way you shift perspectives is a gift one that will serve many
Let life bless you with all its glory and may you share your generosity to uplift others.
My children.. Whenever I lose perspective, you return it to me.

Whenever I forget what truly matters, you remind me.. often without words.
You've expanded my heart in ways no philosophy ever could.

To my life partner, Nirmal..my Jaan, my karmic companion.
We arrived, not to perfect each other but to evolve each other.
Through love, friction, prayer, patience, collapse and rebuilding, we walked through lessons no institution could ever teach.
For every stage we crossed, every truth we uncovered, for every version of ourselves we outgrew together..I am deeply grateful.

I am deeply grateful to Uddhav Kanhai, for his incisive feedback and auditing insight, which allowed me to see this book from an entirely new perspective. His guidance empowered me to revisit and refine the work with far greater clarity and depth.

I'm grateful to my family, my friends, my extended soul-circle, healing companions, my Omi's, each of you played a role in shaping my journey..
Some stayed for seasons, some for lifetimes, some for a moment that changed everything.
Every interaction left an imprint.. Every connection shaped my becoming..

And to my beautiful fur babies, Sushi and Odie.. thank you for the purest love, most innocent form. You remind me daily that joy does not need language and devotion does not need explanation.

Every lesson I have learned.
Every challenge I have endured.
Every transition whether it flowed gently or shattered me open.
Even the moments when it felt as though my soul stepped outside the body, just to breathe.

All of it led me here…

To this point where I am sharing..not from theory but from lived truth.
Not from perfection but from practice.
Not from knowing everything but from having survived enough to listen deeply.

I offer this work with humility and hope, so..
Whatever you are carrying.. feel lighter.
Whatever you are facing.. soften.
And may the guidance within these pages meet you exactly where you are.

Love, Light & Luminous Grace

Gunj

PREFACE

INTO THE ARENA

I didn't stumble into this work. I was pushed by storms I didn't see coming and silences I could no longer bear.

Amid the shadows of everyday life, a drama kept replaying inside me.. a clash of forces older than time, moving through my mind, my relationships, my body, my society, and the wide mysterious fabric of the cosmos.

I call these moments spiritual showdowns. They're not polite debates. They're thresholds… where I'm forced to choose.. stay trapped or rise, numb out or awaken, resist the current or align with it.

This book is the scripture of that journey. The scripture of my soul.

Not theory. Not borrowed wisdom.
Every page here has been lived, bled, wrestled, and transformed in my own being.
At first, I was competing with the planetary pulse…trying to outrun seasons, cycles, demands. At least I thought I was competing with life itself…that pushes and pulls every human into storms of karma, destiny, and choice.

The more I fought, the more I fractured.
But slowly, through fire and silence, I realised there is no real competition.
Then something broke open.

I felt, not with my head but with my nerves and breath, that there was never a race, only rhythm.
The earth breathes in patterns. Energy moves in tides.
My meridians answer to the same music.. from the Root that grounds me to the Crown that remembers God.
The more I fought, the more I fractured. The more I aligned, the more I became.

This book is my map through that alignment.
Not a tidy map.. An honest one..!

What a **"Spiritual Showdown"** Really is!

For me, a showdown is a lived reckoning across three layers,,

Personal: the intimate battleground where self-doubt, fear, past wounds, and quiet addictions try to rule the day. These are the midnight negotiations where I choose belief over disbelief, faith over panic, truth over the old story. These are the crucibles where transformation begins..
Societal: the shared field where injustice and apathy harden into systems. Civil courage, moral clarity, and collective healing are not slogans here, they're spiritual disciplines.
Cosmic: the vast stage of light and darkness, order and chaos. Myth got here first to tell the truth slant: there is a war over meaning. I am not outside it; I am permeated by it.

To walk this terrain I had to accept a simple law..
life doesn't happen to me..it happens through me.
Consciousness is entangled with the universe's energy.
What I attend to multiplies.
What I surrender clarifies.
Synchronicities aren't random; they're handwriting on the wind.
When I listen, they line the path like lamps.

The Competitive Edge, Turned Inward

I used to think "competitive" meant others were my opponents. Now I know: the only contest is with my own inertia. A Competitive Spiritual Showdown is my refusal to drift. It's the daily choice to meet darkness without flinching, to turn resistance into fuel, to forge awareness until it slices clean. Where others hesitate, I step. Where shame hides, I light it. This is not performance. It's sovereignty..the unshakeable centre that no trend, trauma or timeline can buy or bully.

Quantum Connection, Planetary Pulse

Call it mystical or call it physics but when I clean my signal, reality responds. My thoughts and prayers move through me like current; the current moves back. Harmony with the planetary pulse is not passive. It's co-creation: choosing alignment over argument, learning when to yield, when to roar, and when to disappear into silence so the right word can be born.

My Tools, Weapons,and Armour

I learned to fight with what actually cuts:

- Truth that liberates.
- Faith that muscles through the dark.
- Gratitude that shifts frequencies instantly.
- Compassion that heals both self and other.
- Hope that keeps me from collapsing.
- Word of God & Prayer.. strategy, fire, refuge.
- And above all, Energy, the king of weapons.

Flowing clean, it slices through deception and strongholds.

My armour is not metal but discipline…
breath that steadies, boundaries that protect, practices that cleanse, scripture that roots, service that humbles.

Strongholds, Enemies and the Long Game

The enemy rarely shows up wearing horns. It hides as temptation, oppression, deception, false beliefs, and beautiful distractions.

Strongholds can be intellectual, emotional, or cultural..
some are spiritual contracts I never meant to sign.
Breaking them is not only deliverance..it's design work: new patterns for a new life.

This book takes that seriously.
We'll identify the enemy's shapes.
We'll equip using time-tested armour.
We'll pray like people who expect the sky to answer.
We'll engage the world, not with performative outrage but with durable courage.
And we'll stand..because perseverance is warfare's quietest victory.

Why This Isn't Just "Personal Development"

I've faced nights that wanted to swallow me whole, pain thick enough to drown in, confusion sharp enough to cut.
Those nights didn't break me.. they introduced me to myself.

I learned my presence carries a frequency that steadies rooms and opens windows in the soul. I don't do surface-level soothing.
I work at the core..where patterns are born and futures get chosen.
People don't come to me for a temporary glow. They come to remember their power and to practice it.

A Humble Invitation

If you've ever felt the universe brush your skin, if you've ever seen a coincidence arrive with impossible timing, if you've ever known you were made for more than survival..this book is for you.

In thse two volumes. we go through the rhythms (seasons, lunar phases, energy tides) and how they play through your meridians and chakras, from Root stability to Crown connection.

We'll practice mindfulness that actually makes you present,
Gratitude that actually shifts outcomes and
Service that actually heals the field.
We'll step into mystical moments without apologising to logic and we'll come back with instructions for ordinary Tuesdays.

Above all, this tells you the truth: your life is an altar and a battlefield.
The fight isn't with the world.. it's with the lie that says you are powerless in it.
Alignment is not retreat. It is strategy.

Walk with me. Not to admire the view but to move the needle of your destiny.
Bring your doubt… it will become inquiry.
Bring your fear… it will become fuel.
Bring your old names, and together we'll bury them with honour.
Bring your loss to experience the win !

On the other side of every showdown is a re-introduction to your strength, your clarity, your calling, your God.

That's why I wrote this. That's why you're holding it.

What this book will help you do

- Navigate personal battles (self-doubt, trauma, meaning) with practical tools and spiritual grit.
- Engage societal conflicts with moral clarity and compassionate action.
- Contemplate cosmic struggle without losing your grounding in daily life.
- Use prayer as strategy, not superstition.
- Identify deception, dismantle strongholds and stand firm with disciplines that last.

- Align with the planetary pulse, read synchronicities as guidance and co-create without spiritual bypassing.
- Cultivate energetic abundance by clearing frequency blockages in mind, body and field.
- To be introduced to anecdotes that you never fathomed existed.

Walk with me into the realm of Spiritual Showdowns..
where we question what we believe, awaken our inner strength, and discover the deeper forces shaping our lives. This journey is both exciting and eye-opening, calling to anyone who wants to understand the unseen and learn how to work with the power of the spiritual world.
And in a world where these inner battles are often ignored, it's time to bring them into the light.

Step in..
The lamps are lit.
The scripture is open.
And your soul is ready.

"In the arena of the soul, the greatest battles are not fought with swords.. but with the unwavering strength of our spirits in the ultimate spiritual showdown." G³

My journey has been anything but easy.
But instead of breaking me, it **awakened** me.
As a **spiritual warrior, energy activator and healer**, I don't just understand transformation..I embody it.

What makes me different is not just my healing abilities but the depth of my experience, resilience and alignment with divine energy.
My connection to the universe is not just a belief, it's a living force that I have learned to harness. Through my journey, I have become a guiding force for those seeking clarity, those searching for meaning, those desperate to find peace.

I am here not just to **heal**, but to **activate**, to awaken others to their own power. My presence, my words, my energy… it all carries the **frequency of transformation**.
Those who cross my path don't just find temporary relief, they experience
Real shifts.. Real awakenings.. Real breakthroughs..!

Helping you heal on a core level, find your path and reconnect with your own divine power. I am not just another soul on this journey.
I am living proof that pain can become power, confusion can become clarity and struggle can lead to awakening.

Because I have walked that path, I can now help others find their way through it too.

A real connection with the universe isn't light or casual, it shakes you, transforms you, and redefines the way you see yourself and the world. It's not just about calm meditations or rituals; it's about digging into the layers of your own being, shifting how you look at life, and realising you're woven into something much larger than yourself. That's where true purpose and peace are born when the mysteries stop being "out there" and start pulsing through you.

And love.. real love.. demands the same.
You can't skim its surface. You have to step straight into its darkest waters, stand steady when illusions try to drag you under, and hold your ground through the trials it throws.
Only when you let yourself dissolve into the unknown and uncharted, to touch the raw essence of oneness.

"Your soul has been waiting for this conversation.." G³

(..) or (...)

You will notice ellipses appearing after words...
despair... grief... trauma..
They're not decorative nor accidental, they're breath pauses.
Moments where I ask you to slow down.. these pauses exist so the emotion can be felt, not rushed.
In my writing, ellipses are less a punctuation, more a place where the soul exhales...
Where lived experience settles before it speaks again.
When you see them, pause with me. That space is part of the story.

G³ GOONJ

noun | [gee-cube goonj]

Definition

G³ Goonj is not advice, instruction or philosophy.
It is the echo of lived experience.

A G³ Goonj emerges only after a showdown, fears faced, illusions stripped, truth allowed to settle.

What remains is not theory, but resonance: a distilled knowing that the body has lived, the mind has understood, and the soul has accepted.

Derivation

G³ — Gracious · Guide · Gunj

The three dimensions of one voice moving as one:

- Grace that kept her standing.
- Guidance that revealed itself only after collapse.
- Self forged through repeated upheavals.

Goonj ~ An echo after impact…
the soft, steady truth that lingers long after
the noise has fallen away.

AUTHOR'S NOTE

What you're holding in your hands is not just a book.

It's a journey inward raw, unfiltered and unlike anything you've read before..

It's a mirror, a portal, a reckoning..!

Spiritual Showdowns~Scriptures of Soul doesn't teach you who to become, it guides you back to who you were before the world told you who to be.

Unlike other traditional reads, filled with surface-level advice and polished positivity, this journey dives deep into the body's silent memory, the heart's unspoken grief, the mind's tangled patterns, society's quiet expectations, and the soul's ancient aching, longing to belong.

What makes this journey different… is that you won't walk it alone..you'll walk it with me. These pages carry the weight of my own raw, unedited, and deeply unusual. From the ground, from the dirt I've wept in, the fire I've stood through and the cracks I once tried to keep hidden.

The kind that cracked me open in ways no teaching ever could. It's Not just stories wrapped in ribbons, but experiences that shattered me, broke me, stripped me and then slowly remade me from bone, breath, into something holy.

Mind you.. we won't bypass the darkness, here we walk through it, not with fear but with sacred fire.

This book invites you to **feel**, not just fix.

To **remember**, not just reframe.

Through poetic reflections, lived truths, and soul deep insights, there's no attempt to change you.. it dares to reveal you. Each sentence quietly reaches beneath the surface, pulling you closer to the parts of yourself you've forgotten, avoided or buried.

And by the time you reach the final page…

you won't just finish the first book.. you'll find yourself waiting there..!

If you've ever longed for something more real, more soul-stirring, more YOU !

this series, is a homecoming..!

Because this isn't just my story.. It's a mirror for yours.!

Every ache, every breakthrough, every quiet knowing.. from unraveling to awakening is here only for you.

For you to feel less alone in your questions.

For you to see your own reflection in these cracks.

For you to connect, to remember,

and to find your own answers

for that ever-questioning, ever-searching mind.

I don't speak from theory. I speak from thresholds I've crossed.. from nights that emptied me and mornings that rebuilt me. This isn't a curated healing journey. It's a reckoning. A return.

To stop performing healing and start living it.

"Not just another self-help book..a soul map drawn in fire.! G^3

CHAPTER 1

SHOWDOWN WITH SELF

~STAY QUIET.. STAY SMALL.. STAY SAFE..

There was a time, somewhere around 2010, when I walked with fear like it was my shadow.
It never yelled. It never pushed. It whispered.
And I listened.

I lived a thousand silent lives in my head, each one ending in failure, rejection, humiliation.
Not because the world told me I couldn't, but because my own voice did.
The quiet master inside me ruled.
You're too much.. You're not enough..
Stay quiet.. Stay small.. Stay safe..

It wasn't society that caged me.
It was the invisible chain of self-betrayal, forged every time I dimmed my light to keep others shining.

There was a night I won't forget.
In the ladies' room, mid-party, wearing clothes that didn't feel like mine, laughing at jokes that hurt to hear,
performing a version of me that had no pulse.
My stomach clenched. My chest was heavy.
In the cracked mirror above the sink a stranger stared back.

Something snapped.. sharp.. silent.
I gripped the cold edge of the sink and asked my reflection, Who are you, and why have you abandoned me?

That night I stopped performing.
I promised never to betray myself again.
Not for approval.. Not for survival.. Not for belonging..
That was the beginning of my return.

The Lie of if's..

I had called self-sacrifice love.
Saying yes while I was crumbling felt noble. It was not.
Love does not ask you to vanish.

I built a life on other people's blueprints, then wondered why nothing felt like home.
I followed rules I never agreed to. I played roles that drained me.
My biggest enemy wasn't fear; it was the belief that my truth was too inconvenient to live.
I drowned in what ifs..What if I fail.. what if I'm rejected.. what if they leave..
Now I read them differently.
They were code..my mind waving a white flag.

What if it was not weakness.. It was a cry to be heard..
So I stopped judging those doubts and asked them gently..
What do you need from me?
That one question softened everything.

I am not a single story but The multidimensional self
I am Skin and Scar.. Heart and Heat.. Mind and Miracle..
And I'm the one who learned to meet myself on every layer.

Multidimensional layers of self
Physically: My body held the memories I tried to forget.
Emotionally: My grief shaped me but so did my joy.
Mentally: I yearned not just to know, but to understand.
Socially: I longed for spaces that didn't need me to shrink.
Spiritually: I needed to feel I belonged to something greater than pain.

The Body

Physically my body held memories I tried to forget..
But the body never forgets.
Where the mind built walls, the body kept doors ajar.
In the ache of my shoulders lived unspoken burdens.
In the tightness of my chest, the grief I never cried out loud.
In my gut, the silent dread of being judged, left behind, misunderstood.

My skin remembered every moment I flinched but smiled.
Every time I stayed quiet when my soul wanted to scream.
The body is not just flesh it is a library of the unsaid.
It carries the imprints of touch, tone, tension.
Of the moments we wanted to run but froze.
Of the dreams we abandoned to belong.
But in listening to it, truly listening..

I began to unfold..
Each sensation became a doorway..Each pain, a guidepost.
Each breath.. a return..
I peeled back the layers not just of trauma but of truth.
The truth that I am more than what happened to me.
That within the wounded body lives an untamed spirit.
That healing isn't just forgetting, it is remembering who I was before I was hurt.
I am not just flesh and bones..I am memory and light.
Shadow and rebirth..!
And in that realization, I began to open..Into the infinite self.

The Heart

Emotionally, my grief shaped me but so did my joy.
Grief carved me open.

It hollowed out spaces I didn't know existed. It taught me to sit with silence, to bow to endings, to speak the language of loss without words.
But joy ..
Joy came like sunlight after a storm I thought would never pass.
It poured into the cracks, not to erase them,
but to grow something wild and alive within them.

Grief gave me depth..Joy gave me colour..
Together, they sculpted the vast terrain of who I am.
There were days my tears watered the roots of strength.
And nights my laughter echoed louder than my pain.
Each emotion.. a sacred visitor.
Each one.. a mirror and a map.

I realised.. to feel deeply is to live truthfully.
To welcome grief and joy as twin teachers, is to walk the spiral path inward to the raw, untouched places of the self.
I am not just what hurt me and not just what healed me.
I am what bloomed in between.
The infinite self.. layered in feeling, rich in experience, unfolding like a sacred prayer, spoken in the language of the soul.

The Mind

Mentally, I yearned not just to know but to understand.
Facts never fed my soul.. Knowledge was a spark,
but understanding… understanding was the fire.
I didn't want just answers..I wanted meaning.
I wanted to know why I felt what I felt,
why I believed what I believed and why the world moved the way it did.

My mind was a seeker but not of surface truths.
Of essence, of roots, of patterns behind patterns.
I questioned everything Not to rebel but to remember.

To remember what had been buried beneath conditioning, beneath noise, beneath what I had been taught to think.

There were thoughts that weren't mine but lived in me like tenants.
Inherited fears.. Borrowed identities.. and I had to unlearn as much as I learned.

Understanding was a reckoning.!
It asked me to sit with paradox.
To hold light and shadow in the same hand..
To know that clarity doesn't always come clean sometimes, it arrives in fragments, in breakdowns, in quiet moments when the world finally hushes.
And in that silence, layer by layer, a deeper mind awakened.
One that didn't just process but remembered. Not just knowledge but wisdom and when Knowledge softened into wisdom.
The mind aligned with the soul and that alignment became liberation.
In that union, I opened to the infinite self not just a thinker, but a knower of truths felt deep within the bones.

The World

Socially, I longed for spaces that didn't need me to shrink.
Places where I didn't have to trade truth for acceptance, or dim my light just to belong.
I grew weary of rooms that praised my silence but punished my authenticity.
Of conversations that skimmed the surface, while my soul begged for depth.
I craved connection that felt like coming home.. not performance, not politeness but presence.
Where my fullness wasn't too much and my softness wasn't mistaken for weakness.

I began to notice:
I was moulding myself to fit into spaces never built for the real me. I was shrinking in the name of peace, editing in the name of love, vanishing in the name of harmony.
But the cost of fitting in was the slow erosion of self.

So I stopped asking "Do they like me?"

And started asking, "Do I feel safe to expand here?"
''Can I be wild, sacred, messy, whole and still be met?"
And then I finally found those spaces or created them..

Because true belonging isn't found in shrinking.
It's in rising, in standing in your fullness and being held.
In those moments, I stepped out of the disguise and into the infinite self
Unhidden.. unmasked.. unapologetically whole..

The Divine

I needed to feel I belonged to something greater than pain.
Because pain had become a religion I never chose.
A language I spoke fluently, a god I bowed to in silence.
I needed to know that my suffering wasn't sacred
my soul was.
That beyond the trauma, the trials, the endless cycles,
there was a higher rhythm, a divine thread that wove through all things, including me.

I craved more than escape..I craved remembrance..
A return to the eternal within me.
To the knowing that I am not the wound but the witness.
Not the chaos but the consciousness.
I began to see divinity not as a distant force but as breath, as light behind my eyes, as stillness in the storm.

I realised.. even in the darkest hours, something greater had been holding me.
Not punishing me but Preparing me.
For what?
For truth.. For purpose.. For power..

Not the kind that dominates but the kind that awakens.
And in that surrender, I stepped beyond identity, beyond form, beyond fear.
Into the Infinite Self..Where I no longer just belonged to pain.
I belonged to love.. To source..
To all that ever was and all I was always meant to be.

My showdown Decoding my life

To walk this spiral.. the rawness, the grief and the joy, the patterns and the paradox.. was to step straight into fire.

But it was the fire that changed me.
The spark that fed my soul became a flame, and once lit, it did not go out.
Every black hole I crossed, every meaning I craved, every answer I clawed toward, they became a language my soul finally understood.

This was not only the rise of a soul. It was the birth of something fierce enough to bend belief itself.
Only through fire does one rise. Only through ash does one dare call themself a phoenix.

Hence began the decoding of my life..
Not only to break chains but to see the echoes behind them.. patterns behind patterns, traditions and conditioning shaping this specific journey, burdens carried across generations.
Peeling them, I found the deepest source.. the awakening itself.
Mind aligning with soul.. Union of Wisdom with spirit..

The self I had longed for stepping out of the mirror and into my life.

This book is not a gentle diary. It is a map carved out of storms. Every chapter ahead is not proof of survival, but proof of becoming. A vow kept under pressure. A life decoded in fragments.

There are nights & moments that still throb in my bones..

- There was a night when metal walls shook with rain, when fear pressed close enough to choke, and yet, by morning, something vast and unnameable, unclenched a part of me, I thought was gone forever.
- What happened after… let me keep for the page that can bear its weight.
- There was a place, I knelt on, ancient and cold, where sound turned into river and silence into embrace. I walked out of that place not forgiven but re-membered. Now that you've stepped into this space, I will open up gradually.. In the pages that follow, revealing the small but profound moments in their own time..
- There was a circle of laughter & smiles.. light on the surface, sharp beneath. Smiles covered daggers and my silence turned into a chain, I wore for years. What that silence cost me, and what it finally taught me, will come later, when the story is ready to show its teeth.
- And there was a door.. one I opened when I should have run, one that led me into a presence so heavy it shaped years of who I became. I will not name what stood behind it yet. All I will tell you this is sometimes the monsters we fear outside are nothing compared to the ones we learn to live with inside.

These are not stories yet..They are sparks.. Glimpses..
Shadows cast before the fire..The full blaze is yet to come.

G^3 Goonj

So if you choose to walk further, understand this…
this is not entertainment, it is initiation.
Every word ahead is both mirror and blade.
You are not just reading a book. You are entering into a pact. Between my soul and yours. Between what I have kept hidden and what you are now being allowed to see.

I began this chapter with a shadow whispering over my shoulder.
I end it with a different whisper.. the sound of change..
beginning, the quiet glow of metal turning to light.

For years, what healed me last was what I left behind first…my voice.
I had to melt it down to find the truth inside it.
The day I stopped apologising for existing, my body loosened its grip.
The day I named what hurt, grief lost its hold.
The day I set a boundary, my spirit stopped bargaining for worth.

That was my first transformation:
Pain into witness..Witness into wisdom..Wisdom into self.

This is the alchemy I place in your hands now, raw and alive.
You haven't read this before, because I've never written it before.
Every page ahead is a small vial from my soul…
some may burn, some may heal, all will change you.

Hold these first truths like ingredients..

~ Healing is not erasing what happened..it's remembering that you are more than the wound and becoming who you were always meant to be.
~ Self-sacrifice is not gold.. it's lead. Love does not ask you to disappear.
~ Boundaries are not walls.. they're vessels that hold your essence.

~ Grief hollows you so joy can pour in..Together they make you stronger than steel.

This is not just a book.. It's a spell.. A formula..A prayer..
A map carved out of storms.
The more I honoured these dimensions, the more real I became.
Every word is both mirror and blade, solvent and spark.
Each chapter will take something from you and give something back.

You're not just reading. You're stepping into an experiment.
Between my soul and yours.
Between what I've hidden and what I'm about to show you.

Once you step in, there is no unknowing.
Once the vessel is broken, the elixir cannot be poured back.

I am not just body.
Not just feeling..Not just thought.
Not the echo of pain..Not a role someone else wrote.

I am the unfolding..The remembering..The Infinite Self.

Scarred, yes.. Sacred, yes..
Layered in grief, shaped by joy, freed by wisdom, nourished by love.
Not surviving.. Awakening..!

Welcome to the furnace.. Welcome to the work.
It starts at the foundation..quiet and unseen.
It rises with the scaffolding..fragile, uncertain.
It takes form in the walls we build and the ceilings we struggle against, until finally a new height opens..a vantage point.!

Here, at this threshold, the vow begins.
Not shouted.. Not forced..
But steady, like a flame that learns to hold its place in the dark.

CHAPTER 2

SHOWDOWN WITH JUDGMENTS AND PERCEIVED INSECURITIES

Sometimes the deepest betrayals don't come from people who hate you,

but from those who hate how much you remind them of who they could be.. GGG

No matter how good you are..someone will still judge you.

And the hardest part is this.. their judgment has little to do with you. It is a mirror of their own insecurities, their fears, their unresolved pain.

I learned this truth the hard way..This is not a story of petty jealousy.

This is a story of silent sabotage… a fog that lingered for over two decades of my life.

It came not from an enemy but from someone I once called a friend.. A spiritual sister.. A trusted presence.. who prayed beside me, shared my circles, entered my home, even echoed my thoughts. Someone who was meant to rise with me, not against me.

But instead, she stood beside me like a shadow not in support.. but in competition..!

Initially she was kind.. always offered help.. was there for me.. Her pretence unveiled much later in life.. it was only so she can rave to others about it later..

When someone stands beside you long enough, in family, in friendships, in spiritual gatherings, you assume they're part of your journey.

You trust them. You open your world to them. And when that person starts questioning, criticising, competing it doesn't just feel like betrayal. It feels like confusion wrapped in guilt.

That was my experience not for a week, not for a season, but for almost two decades.

She was everywhere.

In my family, she had a place.

In my spiritual group, she was a known face.

In my friendships, she was present and persistent.

And wherever I was invited, She would find a way to shadow it.

The quite war.. at first it was easy to dismiss.

A backhanded compliment here, A glance too cold during my moment of grace, A well-timed interruption when I spoke, A casual tone that made my very name sound like a mistake.

But over time, these weren't accidents. They were patterns.

A pattern of sabotage, not just of opportunities but of my being.

Even in my personal space my home, my heart, my most private struggles her presence somehow lingered..

She had access to too much, and influence over too many.

And almost every interaction I had, whether it was with a new friend, a guide, or a teacher, somewhere her shadow loomed.

If I offered to help at an event, she questioned why I was chosen.

If I contributed quietly, she made sure her voice was louder.

If I was invited somewhere, she found her way there too not to stand with me, but to measure herself against me.

What began as faint cracks grew into a silent erosion.

My joy dimmed, not because my light lost its power, but because I kept dimming it myself for her to shine.

I never questioned my own worth.. but one thought often lingered.

Am I too visible? Should I step back? Should I shrink a little, just to keep the peace?

Shining was not wrong, being visible was not arrogance, and protecting my peace was never selfish.

Yet I understood where she came from.. the scars of marriages that fractured, the weight of balancing two families, the ache of losing her mother, the wounds carved by a father who always dismissed her, the silence of brothers loud as a scream, the neglect of relatives, and the endless echoes of unhealed trauma.

Out of sheer compassion, I stepped back. Not because I felt small, but because I had wounds of my own and the empath in me chose to give her space to breathe.

I knew my light could never truly be dimmed..if it faded in one room, it would rise in another. That was the grace the Divine had placed upon me.

And for years & years, I did.

The Fog of Insecurities

It wasn't just competition. It was corrosion.

She was everywhere in my family space, among friends, in spiritual gatherings, on travel plans, even pilgrimages..

And slowly, her need to "also be seen" became an unspoken rule that others obeyed too.

A whisper here… Why her?

A suggestion there.. Maybe someone else should do it.

A casual dismissal.. Not her.

Each word from her was a stone added to the invisible burden I carried.

And the silence of others made it heavier.

Friends saw. Family noticed. But no one spoke.

Except my husband, who sometimes caught how my spirit wilted. How my energy folded inward every time I was judged in the name of spirituality. With my children she had her halo of niceness on..

And no one said a word.

Except my soul…

But my Soul Refuses to Break

Even when I apologised for my grace, even when I blamed it all on karma, there was something inside me would not bend.

My soul would not bend.. My energy found new shields.

Even when others stayed silent,. My spirit started to speak louder within me.

Here's a truth so few recognize..

You don't need to burn bridges.

Just stop offering your light to those who only want to cast shadows.

And So I Walked On…

Without revenge..Without resentment..Zero confrontations.

Just with reverence for the long road that taught me soul sovereignty.

Torturing my soul was never part of the plan.

I had already walked through fire in this life and where I had reached, it wasn't luck.

It was growth.

It was healing earned..!!

So the last thing I wanted was to sabotage that journey

by staying stuck in a space that no longer honoured it.

so, I did what I knew how to do best.

I prayed to be taken out of the equation altogether. To be lifted from the politics, the passive-aggression, the meek manipulations dressed up as friendship.

I prayed to be released from circles that spoke in whispers, that shrank you when you weren't looking, that bruised you behind your back with words you never deserved.

I was no longer available for spaces that mistook my grace for weakness.

No longer willing to shrink just to be digestible. No longer willing to stay for few hours as an acquaintance with souls I knew for decades and..

where love was just another game of dominance in disguise.

I didn't want to hate.. But I couldn't keep staying where I was quietly being erased.

Because I knew I deserved better.

I deserved peace.. I deserved friendships that nourished, not corroded.

Spaces that aligned with my soul, not silenced it.

And that prayer wasn't a cry for help,

It was a declaration to divinity..!

And so, when her presence pierced me, when whispers multiplied, when even those I trusted echoed her doubts, I turned inward.

My inner light.. the one I had neglected, the one I kept dimming

began to glow multi-folds under suppression.

Faintly at first, it became my compass.

I stopped explaining myself..I stopped shrinking..

I stopped sacrificing my truth to keep false peace.

Instead, I chose myself. Fiercely.

I began to love myself unapologetically.

I guarded my energy like sacred ground.

I started to trust my energy.

To honour my presence.

To tend to my own needs without shame.

To create sacred space around me that no one could intrude upon.

And as I healed, something unexpected happened.

The Sacred Reversal.. Slowly, the tide turned.. People started noticing.

My Guruma.. someone I deeply revered, began to see it too.

The dynamics, the competitiveness, the subtle acts of disrespect it was no longer invisible.

Even a few fellow sufferers shared their bitter experiences..

Despite this there were no interventions, just private affirmation here and there.. enough to remind me that we had endured similar storm. Only to jump in and out of my boat when they pleased...

But a few genuine friends started being vocal too.

It took years.

But her gaze affirmed what I had endured and that small moment of being seen became a turning point.

Not because I needed validation but because I finally understood

It was never about me.

It was always about her pain.. Her lack.. Her fear of not being enough.. She forced her presence to feel whole !

For so long, I lived entangled in someone else's insecurities. I didn't even know I was in a battle because I wasn't fighting one..

Remember.. even your being threatens those who haven't met themselves yet.. so they judge.. They compete.. They sabotage..

Not because you're wrong but because your presence reminds them of everything they haven't yet healed.

Trust me I'm better than that and avoided to indulge in gossip or behind the back talks

And with that came a wisdom..

You don't lose peace by being kind. You lose yourself when you keep shrinking to make others comfortable.

Sometimes the deepest betrayals don't come from those who hate you but from those who cannot bear how much you remind them of what they could be.

Craved spotlight

She wanted to be the one everyone admired, the one people ran behind the star of every party, every gathering, every circle, spiritual or otherwise.

But in chasing applause, she didn't notice, the void she was creating in the most sacred bond of her life. She was sabotaging the only relationship that was real, the only one that wasn't dazzled by her glitter but cared for her soul. Like a sister!

And she didn't even realise it… until it was too late !

Her pain was never mine to heal.. Her insecurity wasn't my failure..

Her judgment wasn't my truth.. Her shadow could never replace my light..

I still love her.. I still respect her.. but I stopped handing her the pen to write my worth.

And when.. the weight became unbearable, I prayed.

Not for her to change.. Not for her to disappear.

But for release..

I prayed to be lifted from the politics, the passive aggression, the whispered dismissals, the meek manipulations dressed as friendship. I prayed for spaces that would nourish my soul, not corrode it. For circles that would honour my presence, not shrink it. For friendships that were not scoreboards but sanctuaries.. not just for me but even for other who had undergone same pain.

And the Divine heard me.. It transformed my path.

It carried me to new zones of existence where I could finally

expand without being sabotaged.

Today, I carry no resentment.. Only clarity and strength..!

Because while she spent years trying to prove herself better than me, I spent years becoming better for myself..

To the One Reading This in Silence

If you too have been judged by someone you love…

If you've been made to feel "too much" by someone in your circle… If you carry invisible bruises from subtle sarcasm, spiritual jealousy, or silent competition…

This is for you..

You are not wrong for shining..You are not arrogant for being visible. You are not selfish for protecting your peace.. You are not their battleground.

You are your own home and their healing is not your responsibility.

But your authenticity is.!

G^3 Goonj

From my wounds came my wisdom, and I leave you with these truths..

~ Do not shrink yourself to soothe another's insecurity.
~ Do not apologise for standing in your truth.
~ Do not hand anyone the power to write your worth.
~ Do protect your energy as sacred ground.
~ Do walk tall, serve sincerely, and shine anyway.

And no matter how good you are, some people will still judge you unfairly

Understand this.. their judgment often has nothing to do with you. It's a reflection of their own insecurities, their fears, their unresolved pain. When people feel small inside, they sometimes try to make others feel smaller too, just to feel a little big of themselves.

When they feel unseen, they criticise those who are seen. When they doubt themselves, they question the worth of others. It's not your fault. It's not your failure. It's not a sign that you aren't good enough.

That's why you have to be careful not of becoming "better" to win their approval but of not letting their wounded perceptions define how you see yourself.

Protect your heart…Protect your truth..!

Maybe they're so full of themselves they might not even realise what pain they're causing.

So Keep growing, keep loving, keep shining even when their eyes are too clouded to see it.

Because your journey was never meant to be shaped by someone else's fears.

It was always meant to be lived freely.. fully.. fiercely.

And no shadow, no judgment, no silent sabotage can ever dim a light that knows where it comes from.

CHAPTER 3

SHOWDOWN WITH ATTITUDE

~WHEN EMPATHY IS MISSING AND YOU'RE THE ONE WHO MUST ADJUST

Attitude is not that grows with time it's engraved.!

It's not that the person has no empathetic bone it's just they've never seen or been through times, the pressure

people go through.. Even within families it's common to find attitude towards others, more due to lack of empathy than understanding.

There's a kind of war we never talk about.
Not the loud kind. Not the kind with fists or fire but the quiet war of attitudes, the stone-faced disregard, the scoffs, the rolled eyes, the snide comments disguised as jokes. The kind of behaviour that forces you to swallow your truth, dim your presence, and walk on eggshells all this is happening inside but you're quite on surface. All for the sake of peace.

They say attitude develops with time.
But sometimes, it doesn't grow it's engraved.
Worn like an armour. Displayed like a badge. Passed down like heirlooms in families where love comes coated in conditions and pride.

These are not people who lack an empathetic bone.

They've just never been cracked open by life.
They've never sat in the heat of pressure, watched their insides shatter, or gasped for breath beneath the weight of survival.
So when you break, they don't understand.
When you bend, they judge. And when you rise, they resist.

When Home Feels Like the Battlefield

Families are supposed to be safe spaces and the power play of attitudes becomes a routine..
But if you've seen attitudes before let me tell you… the most cutting attitudes reside under the same roof.
A sibling's superiority.
A parent's pride.
A relative's passive aggression.
And all the while, you're expected to smile, nod and "adjust."

You're not being dramatic. You're just being…drained.
By the weight of showing up every day and still being unseen.
You try to hold your ground, but how do you do that in an environment where your truth is constantly bulldozed by someone else's ego?
You don't want conflict.
But you can no longer keep sacrificing your peace to avoid it.

Why Their Behaviour Isn't About You

Here's the truth..
Their attitude isn't born from insight..it's born from ignorance… ignorance of experience..!
From not having walked through your fire. From not understanding what it takes to carry burdens they've never known.
And still… mark it .. still you're the one holding space, making room, keeping harmony.

But here's what I want to say to you..

You don't owe your silence to their comfort.
You don't owe your self-respect to their ego.
You don't have to keep making yourself smaller to fit in the frame they've built.

Adjusting Without Abandoning Yourself

Yes, sometimes, we do adjust not because we're weak, but because the situation leaves us no other option.

But adjustment does not mean acceptance of disrespect.
It means choosing yourself within the limits of what's possible.
It means holding your dignity while being the only emotionally intelligent one in the room.

And that? That's not defeat.
That's grace under fire..!

When You're the One Who Feels Too Much

If you've ever wondered why you feel too much, care too much, cry too easily or sense tension others don't even acknowledge.. know this..

Your sensitivity is not a curse.
It's your superpower..!
It makes you aware, present, and deeply human in a world that's forgotten how to feel.
But don't let that sensitivity be used against you.
Don't let their unbothered attitude convince you your emotions are an inconvenience.
Because one day, the same people who mocked your depth will drown in their shallowness.

And you?
You will rise.. Soft.. Whole.. Unshaken..!

Attitude is a choice.
And when it’s laced with calmness and kindness, it can transform everything.

If only people paused for a moment to listen, to understand:
“Where is this person coming from?”
“What weight might they be carrying that I can’t see?”
“They’re only saying so to protect my honour so I don’t get hurt?”

Then the sharpness of conflict would soften.
Walls would turn into windows.
And what once felt like a battleground could become a space for healing.

Empathy isn’t weakness.. It’s wisdom..!

When someone controls their attitude when they choose
Grace over dominance,
Compassion over assumption.. the entire scenario changes. It no longer becomes about winning a moment, but honouring each other’s humanity.

It makes room for conversations instead of confrontations.
It turns interactions into bridges instead of battlegrounds.
It creates relationships where dignity isn’t demanded it’s natural.
🙏

And most family values would be protected and many hurt souls would be unharmed.

Silence…My Power

There was a time when I found myself constantly surrounded by sharp attitudes within family, friendships, even spiritual spaces that were supposed to be safe.
It wasn’t always screaming or cruelty.
It was worse..

The subtle digs.. The eye-rolls.. The dismissals..
The way they'd talk over me, cut me mid sentence, like my words didn't carry weight.
Like my presence was tolerated, not valued.

I'd speak from my heart only to be met with smirks.
I'd share an idea only to be corrected, talked down or brushed off like a child speaking out of turn.
They thought they were being clever.
But.. what they were doing was chipping away at
my spirit.. ..Quietly.. Repeatedly.

I remember one particular evening.
A close circle.. People I once trusted.
I tried to offer a perspective gently, with warmth & concern
But someone cut me off mid-sentence with, 'You always get so emotional, it's not that deep'
The others laughed, I smiled too..nodded.. just to get through it..
but inside, something split.

Not out of weakness..but awakening.
I realised, This isn't about me. It's their discomfort with depth.
Their rejection of softness. Their fear of emotion.
And I was no longer going to pay the price for their
unhealed selves.
So I did something radical that night.
I stopped explaining myself.
I stopped begging for empathy where there was none.
I sat back in my silence not defeated but powerful.

And in that silence, I saw them clearly..
People-pleasing, attention-seeking, chasing fake validations..
That's what they looked like to me.
Like little children, lost in a new school, trying too hard to fit in..
Not realising they were never meant to shrink to belong.

How uncomfortable they were with what I embodied.
How their attitude wasn't personal it was their shield, their limitation.

That moment became a pivot.
From then on, I chose my peace over participation.
I stopped trying to fix, explain or soften their edges.
Instead, I softened mine only inward, only for me.

Because the more I honoured my truth, the less I needed their approval and the stronger I became in my silence.

My Showdown

The Silent Victory…your precious awareness !
You may not always be able to change
the attitudes around you.You may never get the apology, the validation, or even the acknowledgment you deserve.

But the real victory?
Is in knowing you didn't let their bitterness seep into your soul.
You didn't let their coldness cloud your clarity.
You didn't hand over your peace in exchange for their chaos.
Because their attitude, left unchecked, does more than bruise your feelings..it hijacks your mind.

You find yourself replaying their words. Questioning your own reactions. Getting stuck in mental loops, trying to understand why they are the way they are.

How hard is it to really know & respect or even accept the ones you find yourself entangled with,
but all it does is cost you… your mental space, your focus, your health and they remain unshaken.

And that price..? Is far too high..

So here's your way out:

Don't waste your light trying to decode someone else's shadow.
Instead, return to yourself.
They remain the same odd, rude, entitled, uncivilised because that's who they are willing to be.
And yes, you've heard it before: 'People change.'.. But do they ? let's ask the real question:
At what cost.? And for how long will you keep bleeding in the hope that someone else wakes up.?

What is the timeline of that 'change' they speak of.?
Five years.? Ten.?
Two decades of emotional bruises, silent tears, sleepless nights and walking on eggshells?

And even if change does come, will it ever give you back the years that pain stole from you..?
The version of you that you buried just to survive them.

Waiting for people to change is not patience. It's self-abandonment dressed as hope.
And let's cut through the next illusion..
You think your love, your compassion, your healing energy will transform them.

NO..It won't..!

Because people don't change unless they choose to.
Not because you gave more.
Not because you suffered more.
Not because you loved them 'hard enough.'

G³ Goonj

Transformation is not a charity you can offer to someone else's unwilling soul.
So if you're holding your breath waiting for someone to become kinder, softer, more conscious

EXHALE….
Let it go.

Because your mental health is not a payment plan for someone else's delayed awakening.
Your peace is not a sacrifice to be laid on the altar of ..
'maybe one day they'll realise.'

They might or they might never.
We all have our divine timings, our learning..and it may take lives or years to show signs of change
But either way, you deserve peace today.

Not when they change..Not when they apologise.
Not when they finally see what you've been through.
But now…
Reclaim your peace.

Every time someone's coldness tries to pierce your warmth.. Pause.!
Breathe.
Don't react.. Don't mirror.
Just observe.

And the hard one..
Don't Judge…remind yourself, quietly but firmly

'This is not mine to carry.'

Detach emotionally without disconnecting from your values.
Walk away from the noise to protect the quiet within you.
Refuse to let someone else's dysfunction define your day.

Oh, their attitudes will test your peace.
No doubt.
But that test? It's your training ground too..

Draw strength from their chaos not by absorbing it, but by refusing to become it.
Let their bitterness remind you why you choose softness.
Let their rudeness deepen your resolve to respond with respect.
Let their storms show you how deeply you've learned to stand in stillness.

Because in the end..
Your mental health..Your peace of mind..Your emotional balance
That is your true wealth.

And no one's attitude is worth bankrupting your soul.
That will be your real resilience
You were never meant to shrink to fit into someone else's dysfunction.
Remind yourself…
Even in the fire, you were meant to rise not burn but blessed, Not broken but divinely restored.

Your precious awareness !

But here's what I've learnt and what you still can..
Never break a heart just because you can.
For one day, you'll crave the calm I chose
And stand alone where no one knows.

(Where heart broke, Echoes Rose or Pain..cracks soul's echo)
My Rap.. My song..

The voice you tried to silence, found her flame
Steady, quiet, no hurry for fame.

So take this truth and let it burn..
Don't wait for pain to make you learn.

Whispers moved in a softened tone,
She rose with light the stars had known.

Not carved by praise, nor shaped by hands
She rose alone, yet firmly stands.

Not just by the dreamers on the side,
But those who felt her rising tide.
Not just believers but hearts that see
What breaks, what bends, what sets us free.

A force of grace both fierce and deep,
She walked the fire most fear to keep.
She didn't rise to beg or flee
She bloomed through storms and came to be.
not from pride or ache or show
She rose because her roots said grow.
She rose because her soul said so..

CHAPTER 4

SHOWDOWN WITH 'JUST BE YOURSELF'

~WHEN ADVICE IS LOUDER THAN UNDERSTANDING.

We've all heard it…"Just be yourself."

It's the go-to advice.
Before an interview, in a failing relationship, when seeking friendships, when chasing purpose…
"Just be yourself."

It sounds empowering. And sometimes, it is.
But what no one talks about is the other side of this phrase
The shadow side.

Because being yourself in a world that's constantly editing you isn't always liberating.
Sometimes, it's confusing.
Sometimes, it's exhausting.
And sometimes, it feels like a setup.

You try to show up as you, but what does that even mean anymore?
Is it the version of you that people accept?
The one that doesn't offend?
The one that smiles, even when tired?
Or the one that overcompensates with a forced confidence just to survive a space?

This pressure to "be yourself" can backfire.

Instead of grounding you in authenticity, it can create a strange kind of imposed confidence
A mask of certainty that feels more like performance than presence.

And in trying so hard to be,
We forget how to feel. We forget to check in with our truth in that moment. And sometimes, we lose our footing altogether.

Because the truth is
Being yourself isn't a button you switch on.
It's a journey.
And some days, the self is soft, uncertain, and searching.
And that's okay.

For as long as I can remember, I've lived inside the expectations of others.
Family shaping one part of me, society shaping another,
people deciding my tone, my behaviour, even my identity.

Everyone had a version of me, set in their mind.. except the one I was trying to find !
Most people, including my closest even in spiritual circles, wanted a version of me that suited them
But my soul wanted only one thing… to return to myself.
To be me, without edits…

If being yourself were so simple,
the world wouldn't punish truth and reward performance.

It's strange how certain phrases enter your life with good intentions,
yet somehow manage to throw you off track in the most delicate moments.
Just be yourself is one of them.

People say it like it's a soft blanket..

not realising that sometimes it lands like a stone on your concentration.

And, more importantly…
they say it with a confidence that makes you wonder
whether they truly understand you or whether they simply love the sound of their own wisdom.

I remember.. this one evening that thought me what this line actually means.
I was standing backstage, going through my lines for a talk on mental health.
I wasn't nervous.
I wasn't doubting myself.
I was simply… Aligning..Breathing..Preparing…

And out of nowhere,
a friend walked up, tilted her head and said,
"Oh, all the best… just be yourself."

I still remember the exact second
the sentence sliced through my focus.
Just like that, my mind left my lines and started scanning me instead.

Was I looking nervous.?
Did she think I was unsure.?
Why did she feel the need to say that.?
Was she trying to calm me.?
or subtly telling me that I looked like someone who needed calming.?

What was supposed to be grounding felt like being gently nudged off-centre.

One sentence…and suddenly, I wasn't preparing for the stage. I was preparing for her perception of me.

And I hated that shift.
That derailment..That unnecessary doubt..
Oh..I would never want this for anyone

Then there were my spiritual gatherings at my GuruMa's
A room filled with bhajan singers, Carnatic-trained voices,
the kind that reached the ceiling effortlessly.
I knew my hymn..
I knew my sur..
But I also knew they were more seasoned..!

So yes, I had a flutter of apprehension.
Not insecurity...just a respect for their craft.
I was about to sing in Punjabi hymn, a Kirtan close to my heart..
A letter from Guru Govind Singh ji to God..
Just when I was silently tuning my breath, a hand on my shoulder..

"Go on, just be yourself."

Again...That line..That tone.. That unmistakable assumption.

And this time, the shift was sharper..

Why do you think I'm not myself?
Do I look unsure?
Do you see naivety where I see focus?
What are you diagnosing in me that I didn't ask you to read?

The worst part..
The moment they said it,
I wasn't thinking about the hymn anymore.
I was thinking about what they saw in me.
And it frustrated me.. the second time..
not because they said something mean but because they said something meaningless, at a moment that needed meaning.

You know the real problem with advice is that
People assume "Just be yourself" is comforting.

But most times, you're saying:

– You look nervous.
– You look unsure.
– You need reassurance.
– I know better.
– I'm wiser than you.
– I'm more confident than you…

And sometimes, it's more ego than encouragement.
More projection than perception.
Some people extend advice not because they understand you, but because your moment makes them feel important.

And sometimes..
Sometimes…they say it because they have no idea what else to say and don't want to expose their own discomfort.

Either way, it shifts something within you…away from your craft, away from your intention, towards an unnecessary self-audit.

At the confusion it creates when someone says, "Just be yourself," right before you step on stage, right before you sing,
right before you take up space.. it does something subtle and psychological!

It makes you question whether you were being anything else. And in that questioning, your energy splits.

You're no longer present..You're managing perception.
You're adjusting posture.. You're editing your breath.
You're wondering if your natural self looks like someone who needs advice.

That is where the sharpness lies.
That is where the emotional pinch is.

Because I wasn't nervous..I wasn't confused..I didn't need reassurance.
I needed silence.. I needed space.. I needed breath.

Not advice..!

My showdown

So I've learned this…Most people who confidently throw "just be yourself" around are not authorities on identity.
They're authorities on assumption.

Often, they've never been in the space you're standing in.
They've never carried the responsibility you're about to hold.
They've never felt the weight of presence, the vulnerability of performance, the exposure of being seen.

And yet they advise. Boldly..Smoothly…
As if they've mastered the art of being themselves in every complicated room life has ever thrown at them.

But truthfully..?
Some people give advice because silence makes them feel small.

Today, I take that phrase differently..

I don't hear encouragement.
I hear a reminder that people often speak without reading the room, without reading the person, without asking themselves.. whether their words add clarity or create internal noise.

I've learned to protect my energy around such moments.
Because being myself is not a request.
It is not a suggestion.
It is not an emotional responsibility placed on someone else's tongue.
Being myself is my daily discipline..My private commitment..My inner alignment.

And honestly.?

I don't need someone else telling me how to be when they haven't even understood who I am.

This chapter is not about the advice. It's about the impact of the advice.
The timing..The tone..
The assumption behind it..The ripple it leaves in your mind just before you're about to enter an important moment.

I want this chapter to tell the truth..
Sometimes the worst derailments don't come from
enemies, it comes from people who think they're helping.

G³ Goonj

Not every sentence spoken in kindness is useful.
Not every advice-giver is wise.
And not every moment needs a voice.

What I've learned is simple !

Silence is also support.
Presence is also encouragement.
Confidence doesn't always need cheerleading.

Sometimes, the most respectful thing someone can do is allow you to walk into your moment.. with your own breath, your own energy, your own focus.

Because 'your self' is not found in advice.
It is found in the quiet space where no one interrupts your becoming.

"Being yourself isn't always brave or beautiful…sometimes, it's just not pretending anymore." **G³ Goonj**

CHAPTER 5

SHOWDOWN WITH CULTURAL CONDITIONING

~WHEN SILENCE FELT SAFER THAN TRUTH

I didn't always have the courage to walk into a room as myself. There was a long stretch of my life..especially in the early 90s, when invisible social scripts decided everything for me.
What to wear.. How to speak.. What not to say.. Where to pause.. Where to smile.. When to stay quiet..

With no other choice..I learned the rules early..I followed them well..

And yet, something inside me kept tightening.

Social constraints are rarely loud..They don't shout.. They whisper..

They don't chain you but they guilt you.
They don't imprison you but they watch, correct and judge.

They say things like..
Be kind but don't be blunt.
Be capable but not ambitious.
Be educated but not independent.
Be spiritual but don't question tradition.
Be bold but remain acceptable.

And I tried..God knows I tried..!

As adjustment was something I learnt much earlier in life.
I was married at seventeen.

I had just stepped into my twelfth grade when my life was suddenly discussed, decided and distributed
across rooms I wasn't sitting in. After marriage, the instructions were clear..almost administrative.

"You won't need to study anymore."
"And working… that won't be allowed."

There was no anger..No drama..Just certainty.
As if education was something you outgrew the moment you became a wife.

I remember sitting quietly, nodding not because I agreed but because I didn't yet know how to disagree.
In the early 90s, silence wasn't submission. It was training.
Resistance didn't always look like rebellion. Sometimes it looked like waiting.

Fee for another year was already paid, I wanted to pursue college.
Unable to digest the fact what I got myself into I was regretting marrying..
One day during an argument something unexpected happened.
My mother-in-law spoke up.

"No," she said. "She will study. As much as she wants."

Until now.. I had thought of her as an uneducated woman.. someone who had never stepped into a college or a classroom before.
But standing there, watching her take that stand for me, I realised something I hadn't understood before.

She was the only truly educated human being in the room.

That sentence did not come easily.. It came at a cost..

Arguments followed.. Voices were raised..
Resistance came from within her own family but she fought battles I didn't yet have the language or the courage to fight myself.

She fought them anyway. I understood, she was also answerable to the family so the condition remained..
Study was allowed..Working was not..

Since then..education became my only sanctioned form of independence.

I went back to college after marriage.
Regular college.. Day after day..Year after year.
Twelfth. First year. Second year. Third year.

I earned my knowledge in child psychology, physiology, sociology, food and nutrition, subjects that made sense to everyone else.
Knowledge that nurtured.. Knowledge that cared.. Knowledge that didn't threaten..

No one asked what I wanted to become.
But they allowed me to learn how the human body works, how the mind absorbs, how nourishment heals.

At the time, I was grateful.
Only later did I realise..even my education had to be useful to someone else.

I didn't want to study just to pass exams.
I wanted independence.
Money meant choice..Choice meant breath..

But earning wasn't an option, not outside the home, not on my terms.
So I studied harder.
As if knowledge could quietly substitute income.
As if degrees could unlock a door that was currently sealed shut.

Every day, I moved between worlds.
Student..Wife..Daughter-in-law..Sister-in-law..Daughter..!

Books in my bag.. Expectations in my head..
I would sit in classrooms listening to professors talk about growth..mental, physical, emotional and then return to a life where my own growth was carefully rationed.

No one stopped me from studying but no one even asked why I was so hungry for it either.

There was a restlessness inside me that didn't yet have language. I wasn't angry… anger required permission too.
I was alert.. ..Watchful Collecting something quietly..

I learned early that financial dependence doesn't always humiliate you loudly.

Sometimes it trains you to wait.
To plan silently..To store ambition where no one can confiscate it.

And Knowledge became my savings account.
Unusable for the moment.
But untouched.. And entirely mine.

A few months later.. I did work.

But not in the way I had once imagined for myself.
I worked within my husband's company, handling PR.
On paper, it looked acceptable.. Familiar.. Safe..
As I wasn't "working"I was helping.

I answered calls..Managed communication.
Received visitors..Took clients around.
Represented the brand.. Smoothed the edges.
Made business feel easy and possible.

I was in my early twenties.
I hadn't studied emotional intelligence or diplomacy.
No one had trained me in client handling or relationship management. And yet, that was exactly what I was doing.

I managed emotions before I managed emails.
I read rooms before I read balance sheets.

I handled business relationships instinctively...taking their families around, making guests comfortable in unfamiliar cities, checking them into hotels, accompanying them for shopping, organising holidays, lunches, dinners, smoothing personal discomfort, for professional conversations could flow with ease.
I didn't just represent a business.. I held its emotional climate together.

And through it all, I held my image intact..I held my head up high. From the outside, it looked like contribution..
like contentment.. But inside, it felt contained.

I was doing something but never building something that was mine. There was effort but no authorship.
Responsibility with no authority.

Over time, a quiet anger began to collect.
Not explosive.. Not dramatic.. Just compressed.

Marriage came with expectations.
Then children followed.. Then caregiving became central.
Life kept moving forward, ticking off its socially approved milestones, while my own career waited patiently at the back of the room, hand half-raised, unseen.

There were days I couldn't tell if I was tired from work or tired from postponement.

I wasn't resentful of my children or bitter about marriage
itself.

I was bitter about the early marriage.
About how soon my life had been decided.
How quickly my choices had been deferred.
How long my becoming had been put on hold.

I didn't know it then but this pressure…this accumulation of pauses, permissions and delays..wasn't stalling me.
It was fermenting something.

What I called frustration would later become clarity.
What felt like suppression would sharpen into direction.

All I knew then was this..
I was doing everything right..And still, something inside me refused to go quiet.

It wasn't only education or work.

It was clothing.... Voice expression..
I remember wearing an outfit that felt like me..simple, comfortable, honest.
No drama.. No statement.. Just myself..
Whispers followed..Someone laughed..Someone offered a shawl.
I smiled..said nothing and inside, it felt like I had shown my heartbeat and it was deemed inappropriately.

In rooms where my silence was praised more than my ideas.
Where "as a woman" meant I should be softer,
quieter more agreeable.
As if truth had a gender..

My Showdown

My showdown with social constraints did not happen in a single dramatic moment.

It happened slowly.

It happened every time I stayed quiet when I wanted to speak.
Every time I studied when I wanted to earn.
Every time I helped when I wanted to build.
Every time I adjusted when I wanted to choose.

For a long time, I believed suppression was holding me back. That the pauses, permissions and delays had cost me time, confidence and direction.

But with time, I began to see the truth.
Nothing was wasted.

Every subject I studied taught me how the human body responds, how the mind absorbs, how emotions settle and surface.
Every role I played trained me to read people, sense moods and understand what remains unsaid.
Every conversation I managed sharpened my awareness of energy, power and emotional undercurrents.
Every emotion I learned to read taught me the patience to listen without interruption or judgment.
Every relationship I held together taught me resilience.. the kind that stays present without breaking,
to remain steady even when things felt uncertain

Even my silence was training.
It taught me patience…It taught me listening.
It taught me how to stay present without needing to perform or please.

What I once called delay was actually preparation.
What society would name as adjustment, life was quietly turning into preparation.

The discipline.. The patience..The emotional intelligence..
The ability to hold space, read people, sense what wasn't being said.

By the time I stepped into my own work, my own voice, my own path as a healer, nothing felt unfamiliar.
I didn't need to learn how to hold space…
I had been holding it my entire life.

Social constraints that tried to contain me..instead, they gave me depth. All of it was training me for a path I didn't yet know how to name.

They pushed me inward until I learned how to sit with discomfort…mine and others.. without judgment, without fear, without needing control.

My showdown was not about breaking rules.
It was about outgrowing them.
And choosing, finally, to live from truth instead of permission.

G³ Goonj

If you grew up learning how to adjust before you learned how to choose, this is for you.

Not every delay is a denial.. Not every pause is failure.
And not every form of suppression destroys you.
Sometimes, it shapes you quietly.

Ask yourself without blame..

What did I learn while I was waiting.?
What skills did I build while I was adjusting.?
What awareness did survival teach me.?

Your silence was not weakness. Your compromises were not stupidity. Your longing was not pointless.
They were signals.

The moment you stop judging your past as lost time, you will begin to see the preparation hidden inside it.

And when you finally step into your own path whether as a healer, a creator, a guide, a mentor or simply a more truthful version of yourself…you'll realise this:

You were never behind..You were being prepared.

Social conditioning may shape the outer chapters of your life but they do not get to decide your inner direction.

That choice always comes later.
And when it does..it comes with clarity, strength and calm knowing.

Social constraints didn't break me..They refined me..!

They pushed me inward until I learned how to listen deeply. They delayed my voice until it carried weight.
They suppressed my choices until my direction became undeniable.

I didn't arrive at healing by accident.
I was shaped for it through silence, study, service and survival.

Conformity may win you acceptance. But authenticity wins you alignment.

And alignment, eventually, leads you home.

CHAPTER 6

SHOWDOWN WITH EXTERNAL VALIDATION

~THE HOLLOW BUCKET

Seeking external validation is like trying to fill a bucket with a hole at the bottom.
No matter how much approval we pour in, it always seeps out, leaving us hollow and thirsty again.

For years, I didn't realise I was living with that hole. The need to be seen, appreciated and acknowledged was so subtle, so socially acceptable, that it felt natural even righteous. But beneath it all lay a quiet fatigue, the exhaustion of living for applause that never stayed.

External validation is an invisible addiction..
It disguises itself as love, duty, excellence, and ambition. It promises worth but delivers dependence.
And I, unknowingly, was its most obedient disciple.

My young life was built on dreams that touched every horizon, from becoming a doctor, a lawyer, an actor, even a prime minister.
My imagination was vast, my ambition relentless.
But at seventeen, marriage arrived like an unexpected detour.. tender, traditional, and demanding.

Encouraged by my mother-in-law to learn and study, I was also gently promised that my role would never extend into becoming a "working woman."

Out of respect and love, I agreed and chose obedience over rebellion.
Learning became my refuge. Knowledge became my world.

I pursued my education in Food & Nutrition, Sociology, Psychology, and Physiology, driven by a thirst that never dimmed. I built a home that thrived on care, devotion, and quiet excellence. I found joy in nurturing, organising, and creating but deep down, there was a quiet ache.

Despite my insight and wisdom, I was often overlooked corrected, dismissed even unheard buy so called working women/ achiever's I had as friends and by also by my own people.
My light shone bright but always behind someone else's shadow.
I kept hoping that one day… my intellect would be noticed, that my worth would be validated by the people I served and the world I stood among.

And so began the long, unspoken affair between my soul and external validation.

This was the beginning of inner restlessness..
In conversations, I often found myself shrinking not from lack of confidence, but from the conditioning of invisibility.
My wisdom poured into nurturing others, yet I remained the silent listener, the unseen giver.. someone who made chai or a snack for the ones who stayed after party chatting and laughing without missing my presence.

The world rewarded noise, not depth.
And so..I yearned to be acknowledged, to be included, to be heard..!

Each time someone praised me, it felt like oxygen.. as if by my life had meaning..
Each time they didn't, it felt like I was fading.

That was my inner conflict… a lifelong tug between the woman who knew her worth and the girl who still waited to be told she was enough.

Then came **Kailash** not as a trip, but as a summon.

It was as if the Divine itself whispered,
"Come now, let the mountain speak where no one else has."
After seven days of relentless travel from Kathmandu to Tibet, battling nonstop cold rain, narrow ghats, landslides, and the furious Brahmaputra, I reached the mystical land that seemed to hum with ancient breath.
Each obstacle the stranded vehicles, the broken roads, the freezing winds was an initiation, stripping away layers of identity and expectation.

My soul-travellers, My friend Minku and twenty-one pilgrims from across the world, guided by Swami Mahesh, we stopped to acclimatized at Darchen.
Thers more to this story which I'll share another time.

Each of us cloaked in yellow ponchos, laughing through the sharp rain as if childhood had returned. Laughing, singing, mingling, clicking pics with local Tibetans, so effortless.

The next morning, we reached Mansarovar, the celestial lake believed to absolve sins and purify lifetimes of karma..
There was an unexplainable magic..
The wind there had a voice, the water a memory..

It was freezing.. I somehow removed shoes and layers of socks and as I walked through the ice chilled slippery pebbles into the freezing water…something inside me burned awake.. A feeling… A vibration.. so Alive ..!
It is believed that bathing and drinking this divine water one becomes fortunate and clears all his sins.

As rain continuously drizzled into our Havan fire, we chanted 108 times the Maha Mrityunjaya Mantra..
While our spiritual offering of the sacred mixture of dried herbs, roots, flowers and many aromatic and purifying natural ingredients, into the fire.. we, sitting around the fire in that biting cold, cladded in layers of clothing and down jacket, was indeed a blessing..and the smell of herbs burning in the sacred fire was something else..
a smoke purifying and cleansing the environment and one breath of it and you're no longer present but transported to another realm somewhere between breath and divinity..

The fire danced in defiance of the rain. The flames rose as the water from heavens poured and I remember thinking…This is how grace works contradicting yet in perfect harmony.
It still gives me chills to think about this day how we were able to perform havan on the shore of the lake while rain fell continuously into the fire, continuously obstructing it..

After an early soulful dinner at Mansarovar cafeteria everyone retired early after the tiring day..
We stayed overnight at the aboard on the shore of Mansarovar lake.
That night, sleepless and shivering with the draft coming from the broken window…I gazed from a cracked window at the lake. Through the mist, I saw sparkling streaks of light descending into Mansarovar a vision so divine it felt forbidden..shades of pastel green and warm white..ethereal!

Weather was freezing and we were advised not to step out to explore the ancient theory… They say gods descend here at night to bathe in astral forms and we must not intrude their sacred space

So I did not step outside, despite the ban, the vision
entered me.

The divine no longer needed my movement..it wanted my stillness.. it appeared to me through that cracked window showing me its glory for a few minutes that felt like infinite.. As if I was being welcomed at the gates of heaven with subtle yet magical firework descending from up above.!

The next day, after a few hours of bus ride we arrived at Yam Dwar (the Gateway to the heavens).
One must cross this small temple like gate before beginning the Parikrama, the sacred walk around the mountain.

And beyond it lay Dirapuk and the North Face of Kailash.
Nothing…not scripture, not imagination, not innumerable browsing could have prepared me for that sight.

The mountain stood.. timeless…like eternity incarnated..
The play of light & shadow across its face shifted from gold to silver to starlit shimmer… while Clouds danced around it like celestial messengers.
And I stood… transfixed.
I didn't know if I was crying or praying… a captivating feeling in that moment..

For hours, I could not move.. I felt something burst open in my chest…a warmth rising from my spine, spreading through my back, turning into tears.
It was as if my soul had stepped out of my body to
embrace the mountain and the mountain willing to embrace me back.
Every nerve hummed with music..
Every gust of wind carried whispers of home.
suddenly, I knew… I had not come to Kailash, it was all a divine play..
Kailash had been waiting for me..

By seeking humbly permission to climb, as I started the parikrama of Kailash.
It started to unveil itself.. After quite a steep incline, of a few hundred feet higher, towards the North Face of Kailash.. We meditated as a group sitting on the grounds of mountain.. Eyes closed…Breath steady.. for over an hour in that sharp drizzle… the mountain disappeared..!!

And appeared a vast energy…Shiva Himself !
Sitting in this huge form with open palms laying on each other on his lap.
Majestic..!
Eyes heavy with compassion..
From His crown flowed Ganga and I could feel its gentle stream upon my head… soft, golden, purifying, relieving..
And I, in his majestic palms, gazing at his calm eyes..

As humans we can hear heartbeat if we lay close to someone's chest and for me I could hear this unusual hum like sound that surrounded Shiva's aura and I was experiencing this from inside of his aura…

In that precious moment, I understood the essence of silence..
That validation from others is noise and validation from within is Naad, the eternal music..sound of universe.

Tears poured continously from an hour were camouflaged by rain. When I finally opened my eyes, the tears that rolled down my face were not of sorrow but release.
The mountain was no longer outside me.
It had taken residence within.

It felt like my soul unfolded there and then again rose to the peak of emotions and back into the present body

It's difficult to describe this feeling in words..

Something popped out from the middle of my chest and merged with the gorgeousness of the mystical mountain and I felt a flush of calming sensation in my spine… a chilling as well as warm sensation in the lower region of my spine and it spread into my entire back giving me chills and goosebumps.. b
Best described as a strong vicks vapourab applied on my lower back and due to freezing weather felt like chills.
It was all very communicative.. in a very musical way as if some kind of energy was filtering through all impossible realms and reaching out only to me..

so I can hear the music, the song…
Trust me when I say this… all this while I felt I'm going closet to Kailash in this journey of mine but in actual the mountain was waiting for me..
Ohh it was beyond special..Precious !

Absorbing what I felt while standing upon the precipice of the world..
A realisation began to crystallise within me. The vast expanses of the of the highest peaks around me, amplified the whispers of my innermost thoughts, enveloping me with tranquility.
As I closed my eyes to seep deeper into this experience, a sense of self and purpose ignited within me and I found myself beautifully shedding the weight of external
validations and embracing myself with the undeniable depth of my own wisdom.
I developed a newfound understanding and recognising the journey of my life, that even the insignificant moments held a significance of its own.
The moments of being overlooked and countless instances of being corrected, paled against the revelation that my purpose is not to seek validation from others but to nurture the light of wisdom that resided within me, all along !

As the stubborn, misty, wet weather was overpowering, the winds whispered timeless secrets and the giant peaks stood witness to the resilience of nature, I finally embraced the core of my being and My life's experiences, fluttered with moments of humility, striking a spiritual epiphany, giving me a spine chilling feeling that merged with my understanding and resonated with me.
Ohh.. IT WAS ALL SO MIRACULOUS !

Suddenly all changed…the winds grew fierce and we planned to descend immediately. As we descended, The weather turned stormy.. entire mountain engulfed by dark clouds and rain trying to shift into a storm..
But I was calm as if cradled in the lap of the Mother.

I realised that every moment of being overlooked, every correction, every invisibility.. was a preparation..
They were chiseling me into clarity.
My purpose was never to be seen by the world.. it was to see myself…fully, truly, divinely.

The validation I had chased for decades could not compare to the whisper I heard from the mountain that day
Communication was clear..
"You are not the echo of applause.
You are the sound of consciousness itself."

Finally we reached back to our metal containers that we were staying in waiting for the weather to slow down..

And once it did..
we went to a monastery were Buddha had meditated in a cave and monastery was built around it.
We spoke to the monks… prayed with them..
As monks chanted as we meditated in quiet communion..I was in some otherworldly charm and my true mantra was now silence.

All I could think or hear was the music of winds whispering to me the most beautiful song I've ever heard.....

Entire journey of 7 days back to Kathmandu.. I could hear the winds singing, the mountain breathing and
my soul smiling...

I returned from Kailash no longer hungry for acknowledgment.
My presence, once overlooked, now radiated quiet assurance.
My voice once hesitant became soft yet anchored.
The world had not changed...I had..!
And in that shift everything changed.

The Showdown

The real showdown wasn't against others who failed to see me.
It was against the part of me that forgot her own light.

At Kailash, I faced the hollow bucket, the endless need to be filled by others' praise and watched it dissolve into the lake of self-acceptance.
In that mirror-like water, I saw not the reflection of a woman waiting to be validated but the face of a soul already whole.

The applause faded..The noise quieted..
And all that remained was radiant light...mine.

G³ Goonj

External validation is like borrowed light, it warms you for a moment but it cannot sustain your flame.
True validation begins when you stop seeking mirrors and start becoming the sun.

Kailash didn't give me recognition it gave me remembrance. It reminded me that no mountain, no person, no word can grant what already flows within.

When the world overlooks you, smile gently.. as it's life's way of redirecting your gaze inward. And once you see your own brilliance, even silence will start applauding.

Upon my return from that sacred peak, I carried with me a sense of self that transcended beyond the need for external recognition. I found solace in the gentle strength of my spirit, rooted in humility, drawn from the wellspring of profound experiences.
My presence, once overlooked and oftentimes overshadowed, now exuded a serene confidence, grounded in the unshakable understanding of my own worth and purpose.
Each step I took, as if guided by the profound echoes of the sacred mountain, vibrating with firm truth of my worth and purpose are unbound by short lived validations of the world.

This transformative journey has guided me to overcome the overwhelming need of approval from others has allowed me to live a more authentic and fulfilling life.
With the reflection of my inner light, I started drawing others to my gentle wisdom and unassuming grace.

Though Challenging on the external, this journey within guided me towards the deeper layers of self-realisation and spiritual enlightenment.
This mystical journey holds a great deal into my transformational experience, purifying my soul and paving the path towards spiritual awakening, unraveling deeper insights and truths about my life and existence. I experienced a strong sense of physical and emotional healing with a few divine encounters, amidst the peaceful sacred landscape.

This journey to Kailash Mansarovar, made me realise that seeking external validation was not only exhausting but also detrimental to my sense of self-worth.
From that moment on, I made a conscious effort to trust my own instincts and seek validation from within, rather than relying on

others to validate my choices. This shift in perspective has greatly improved my confidence and
self-esteem… I felt more empowered to pursue my own path without constantly seeking approval from others.

I began to find fulfilment and confidence in my role in life as I had discovered a newfound sense of respect and
appreciation for myself as a important contributor in my family's life.
The journey to unshackle myself, from the craving of external validation, granted me a profound sense of liberation and self-assurance, enabling me to manifest a life where my voice was celebrated for its unique insights and wisdom.. and all this happened with the sacred touch of Shiva and the sound of eternal hum that still vibrates within me🙏

CHAPTER 7

SHOWDOWN WITH UNWORTHY

EFFECTS OF NEGATIVE WORDS

Frustration or lack of words in an lengthy baseless argument usually causes a person to speak negative harsh words.

Social criticism can be a valuable tool for identifying and addressing societal issues, but it is important to approach it with an open mind and a willingness to learn and grow. It can be easy to take criticism personally, especially when it pertains to deeply ingrained beliefs or practices. However, when we approach social criticism with a positive mindset, we can use it as an opportunity for self-reflection and growth.

Negative words struck a deep chord

A women close to me, had dedicated herself to being a homemaker and raising her children with unwavering love and care. As her children grew older and more independent, she expressed a desire to enter the workforce and pursue a career. As her family was facing major financial challenges, she wanted to step-in to take some pressure off from her spouse. However, during her first few job interviews, her harsh encounters with interviewers who made comments that subtly undermined her confidence and experience in the professional world. Some even insinuated that her years as a homemaker had left her ill-equipped for a successful career,

suggesting that her skills were outdated and that her time spent at home was a sign of incompetence in the workplace.
And they doubt if she's capable of the commitment. Her close friends advised her to keep enjoying life as a homemaker as in her mid 40's she won't be able to sustain the work pressure.
Such negative words struck a deep chord within her, shaking her self-esteem and causing her to doubt her own capabilities. She began to question whether she could truly compete in the job market after dedicating herself to her family for such long years. The hurtful remarks echoed in her mind, breeding feelings of inadequacy and uncertainty about her worth in the professional sphere.

Despite the de-motivation, setbacks, sep-doubts and hesitancy, She didn't give up. She sought out a few genuine people from her supportive networks, hired skilled staff, Personally trained them and refused to let those negative words define her, instead she turned the criticism into a catalyst for her growth.
She decided to open her own boutique in the space that was locked for years as an dead investment but on a prime locality. Whatever she could afford to start her own business, From selling her priceless possessions, to saree's in her wardrobe and some pieces of fabrics stored in bags for personal use, she used them all and created an elegant, eye-catching, fusion collection of Indian festive & party wear, a few in bridal collection and some real classy co-ord sets that left buyers asking and craving for more. With no competition in that locality she was thriving in her creative work and it didn't take long for her hard work to be noticed by young designers from the Indian Film Industry and few from overseas.

From new launches, birthday gatherings, music launch, to personal affairs like wedding and house parties, her collection kept soaring popularity among the Indian celebrities, TV stars and many Page 3 personalities, they personally walked into her store just to own her collection.

She impressed many female actors from yesteryears like Nanda ji, Waheeda Rahman Ji, Rekha Ji to Sridevi, Karishma Kapoor, Kareena Kapoor, Urmila Matondkar, Sushmita Sen to name a few, with her unique designs, this made her extremely demanding in the Global Indian Fashion market. Small boutique owners in UK ,USA & Dubai also became her regular buyers.

Thriving in this new role, with her unique personality, a perfect blend of empathy, organisational skills she was known for her problem solving abilities and respecting the on-time delivery constraints. That she had honed during her years as a homemaker. Her resilience and perseverance not only led to her professional success but also inspired her to advocate for other homemakers seeking to re-enter any workforce.

My brave Mom's journey marks the life-changing power of negative words and the lasting impact they can have on one's sense of self-worth while also serving as an evidence of strength of the human spirit and the transformative potential of Hard work, Resilience and self-belief.

Her story is a reminder that every individual possesses valuable skills and experiences, regardless of their background, and that no one should be made to feel incompetent based on their choices or life circumstances. It's a call to be mindful of the words we use and to uplift and empower others on their unique paths to success.

One way to approach social criticism, in a positive light, is to see it as an opportunity for growth and improvement, a path successfully chosen by my mom.

Instead of becoming defensive or dismissing the criticism, we can use it as a chance to examine our beliefs and behaviours and consider how we can contribute to positive change. This can lead to a greater understanding of the issues at hand that need instant focus and a more constructive approach towards addressing them.

Another key aspect of taking social criticism positively is to recognise that it is not a personal attack. Criticism of societal structures or practices is not a reflection of an individual's worth or character, but rather an examination of orthodox systems and patterns. By separating the criticism from our personal identity, we can view it with a clearer mind and a more open heart and gain success and fame in any field just like my mother did. I take immense pride to share this, as in her time, when she started her business, there was no social media or marketing agency helping her grow but purely her passion and dedication to grow in her career made her popular in the Indian Fashion Industry.

Gaining access to unique ideas or perspectives

In order to take social criticism positively, it is important to approach it with humility and openness. This means being willing to listen to different perspectives and acknowledging that we may not have all the answers. It also means being open to making changes and taking action to address the issues that have been brought to our attention.

Social criticism can be crucial for addressing societal issues, but it is important to approach it with a positive mindset. By seeing it as an opportunity for growth, recognising that it is not a personal attack, and approaching it with humility and openness, we can use social criticism as a tool for positive change.

Unlike.. My brave Mom, I've suffered largely coping up with harsh remarks, negative remarks and personal comments and sacrificed most precious prime years of my life for some miracle to happen. It took many years and struggles to make me realise that while it may be uncomfortable to receive negative feedback, but on a personal level, When individuals approach new ideas and feedback with an open mind, they create space for learning and growth. It enables them to explore different viewpoints, challenge their own assumptions, and expand their understanding of the world.

With Open-mindedness, came new ideas,
new perspectives, and feedback with a willingness to learn and adapt.
I mainly realised, accepting criticism is an essential part of self-improvement, as it provides valuable insights and opportunities for development.
Now I take these harsh words to serve as a catalyst for personal and societal growth by shining a light on issues that need attention and by challenging individuals and society to self-reflect and improve.

My Showdown

My real showdown was not with people who spoke harshly.
It was with the authority.. I unknowingly gave their words.

I realised that unworthy words only become dangerous when they are accepted without examination.
Every time I stayed silent, tolerated dismissal or waited for validation, I was quietly agreeing with a narrative that was never mine.

This showdown taught me that resilience is not about enduring negativity.
It is about deciding which voices deserve access to my inner world.
The moment I stopped internalising criticism as truth and began viewing it as information, the power shifted back to me.
That was the moment I reclaimed my self-worth.. not by proving anything, but by choosing discernment.

G³ Goonj

If words have ever made you shrink, pause here.

Not every opinion deserves a permanent place in your mind. Not every voice qualifies as a guide.

Harsh words can either become prisons or pathways..the difference lies in your awareness.

When you stop absorbing unworthy criticism, you don't become rigid.. you become rooted.

Let feedback inform you, not define you.
Let experience speak louder than judgment.

And remember…your worth was never up for debate.
Bear in mind, My personal take from past adversities is that, accepting criticism is a sign of maturity and self-awareness.

Gathering feedback from a diverse range of sources can spark creativity and innovation. Exposure to different ideas and approaches can inspire individuals to think outside the box, explore new concepts and adapt their strategies in unique ways. Which further fosters intellectual curiosity, creativity and a willingness to embrace change and helps individuals build stronger relationships, as they are better able to appreciate the experiences and perspectives of others.

When we're open to varied perspectives, our personal and professional growth becomes deeper and more balanced.

CHAPTER 8

SHOWDOWN WITH THE SILENT STIGMA

~THE CONTROL THAT WEARS A MASK

There was a time when I thought silence was strength.

That swallowing my tears, stitching my lips, and carrying the weight of someone else's control without protest was the mark of a "good woman."
A good daughter.. A good wife.. A good mother..

But silence is not strength.
Silence is a slow poison.

Stigma >>Mental Health Neglect
The stigma around mental health is the cloak that hides it, the accomplice that lets this poison seep deep into our veins until it begins to rot the soul.

On the surface, everything looked fine.
A family, a partner, a home, a life woven together.
Smooth, almost enviable.
But the truth? Smooth… until it wasn't.

I lived in a relationship that demanded my silence as its currency. A control that didn't always shout, but dictated.. how I dressed, where I went, who I met, how I laughed, how much I spoke.. even how I breathe inside my own home.

As I was very young to step into the institution of marriage

I never realised or saw the signs..
I was so madly in love and engrossed in my marriage.. it was my world.. something I had always dreamt, growing up watching Indian movies.
And I would go any length to fix things..!

So it started with small dismissals..
I would try to give an opinion about finances, work related, about parenting, about family issues and I would hear words that cut deeper than a knife!

"You don't have brains."
"Keep quiet.. I just want to share I don't need your opinion or advice."
"You stay at home all day, you don't know how the world works."

That's how patterns are born..!
Not in one grand act of domination but in the thousand tiny ways a voice is silenced.
Without realising… we women allow the pattern to continue until it becomes habit.
Until silence becomes our second skin. Until the men who enforce it, in name of marriage, no longer even realise how much patience they are testing, how many wounds they are carving, how serious of a storm they are suppressing or what they're creating in someone's mind.

~ Creating a sense of dismissal
~ Being disrespectful
~ Leaving one feeling..
unwanted..unimportant..unappreciated !

The Night that Broke me..
This one night I cannot forget. It was not a fight, not a
physical blow just another dismissal.

I had dared to share a suggestion about how to react in a certain situation .
And the reply came sharp, almost routine..
"You don't know anything. Stay out of it. Don't try to teach me. Entire world learns from me.. You're home the whole day, what do you understand how the world operates..?"

That was it. A sentence he probably forgot within the hour.
But I didn't..
That night I lay in bed with tears streaming silently, my chest aching as though my ribs were breaking from
the inside. I cried until my body convulsed, muffling the sound in the pillow so the children wouldn't hear.

It wasn't the first time. And it wasn't the last.
But that night, unraveled me.
I realised I wasn't upset for that one insult..
I was crying for every "keep quiet" that had piled up over years, for every opinion I had buried, for every dream I had folded and hidden away.
And the cruelest part..?
Next day, I woke up, wiped my face, wore my smile and indulged into the routine as though nothing had happened. Because I had learned the art of covering bruises with
forgiveness.

But the mind remembers..The body remembers..
The soul keeps a ledger of every suppression, every wound, every stolen breath.

I wasn't crying, I was choking on my own existence.
It wasn't a sob, it was a strangled scream lodged inside my chest.
Every breath tore through me like shards of glass, as if my lungs had forgotten how to keep me alive.
It felt like death had moved in.. not the death of someone else, but the slow execution of me.

Piece by piece..Breath by breath..I was burying myself alive in that silence.

And the cruelest part beside me, in the same bed, he slept.
Unmoved...Unaware..!
Blind to the fact that with every careless word, every dismissal, every cut to my spirit.. was not just silencing me.
He was unmaking me.

And next day, the cruelest charade.
A casual "Hi, my love", as though nothing had happened.
I if I ever dared to confront.. he would say how much he loves me and he never meant to hurt me and things like this was normal in a married couple.

As though he hadn't watched me collapse inside myself the night before.
As though my breakdown, my gasping, my soul's trauma could be erased with a smile and a morning's kiss.

And I… I always played along.
I forced the smile. I whispered back the words.
Sometimes only a nod.. Yes, everything's fine.
This is my life.. This is my family.. This is love..
I tamed myself.. things happen.. move on.

As I wipe the hurt though nothing had happened. The art of covering bruises with forgiveness, emerged.. don't know how and from where..? But I mastered it..

Most times forgiveness came so easy to me like hail falling relentlessly in a storm, sudden and heavy, leaving dents no one cared to see.
And sometimes forgiveness was like ash after fire , silent, weightless, covering everything in grey, leaving grey dust behind and hiding the burn that came before it.

And every time I forgave, I thought I was healing.
But in truth, I was only burying the evidence of my pain under layers of silence.

What no one talks about is that..
We are feeding an illusion that this behaviour is normal, that this cruelty has no consequence.
And once that seed takes root, it grows into something almost irreplaceable.

Without a slight hint.. emerges and encourages a narcissist behaviour.
This was all the price of silence !

The Long Years of Silence

Three decades of silence is not silence at all… it's a scream buried alive.
It twists your identity. It makes you an introvert even if you were not born one.

As a child, I was already weighed down by challenges that never let me feel free.
As a teenager, I learned to shrink my voice.
As a young bride, I learned to bend until my spine nearly broke.
As a mother, I learned to disappear so my children could shine.
Made room for friendships to bloom..

And when all these years add up, the result is not just "a woman who endured."
The result is anxiety carved into your bones.
The result is depression disguised as devotion.
The result is a thousand illnesses creeping through your veins.. felt in your bones.. not always seen but always felt.

That is the violence no one talks about !
The violence inside the body when the soul has been

silenced.

And here is the cruelest twist…
Even when you break, even when your heart aches to cry for help, society teaches you to hide it.

Go to a gynaecologist..? Acceptable.
Go to a dentist..? Share it openly.
But go to a therapist..?
Hide it.. Whisper it.. Deny it..

We live in a culture that says, "Don't overthink. Be positive. It's all in your head."
And this is how this stigma blocks healing.

But no one sees, those words are not medicine they are another form of stigma.
They dismiss the pain, delay the healing and push the wound deeper until it festers into something irreversible.

No one whispers about a broken leg. But everyone whispers about a broken mind.
And that whisper, that silence, is the real disease.

The Healer's Revelation

For the longest time I believed my silence was protecting my children.
I thought if I swallowed my words, if I muffled my cries into pillows, they would never know.
But children don't just hear what you say they feel what you live. They see the lowered eyes, the trembling hands, the smile stretched too thin.
And they grow up carrying those impressions like invisible blueprints..
Daughters learning to endure what their mothers endured,
Sons learning to dismiss what their fathers dismissed.

Silence does not protect children it infects them.

And this wasn't just in my home.
There were the voices of the world around me
well-meaning aunts, in-laws, neighbours, even friends..
"Adjust, compromise, that's how marriage is."
"Don't complain, everyone goes through it."
"You want respect..stay married."
And above all, a mother's voice echoing like a verdict…
"You're welcome to visit us as a couple."

Every phrase was another nail in the coffin of my voice.
It wasn't just one man silencing me.. it was an entire culture that rewarded my endurance and punished my truth.

And still, I kept telling myself it was strength.
It was love.
But every time I forced a smile and said, "Let's move on,"
I wasn't forgiving him..I was betraying myself..!

Every move on… was another layer of dirt thrown on the grave of the woman I used to be.

But there came a moment sharp as lightning, undeniable as truth..when I whispered to myself:
"No more silence.. No more narcissist manipulation..
No more letting my soul rot while I call it love."

That whisper was not anger. It was the first breath of my healing.
The day I chose to honour my voice, trembling, breaking, was the day I began to rise from the grave of my own suppression.
Because suppressed emotions are like lava beneath the earth, ignored for years, building, swelling, until one day the ground splits open and fire devours everything in its path.

That's what happens when you bury yourself alive in
silence.

The eruption comes… if not in words, then in illness,
in breakdown, in rage.
Silence is never harmless. It always explodes.

Here is the truth I learned too late..
In house narcissists are not born fully grown.
They are fed.. Fed by silence.
Nurtured by every time we pretend things are fine.
Made strong by every time we let them cut our sentences, dismiss our worth, rewrite our reality.
Narcissism grows on the soil of our silence
And then it towers so tall, it shadows our entire life.

Today, I am not the same woman I was.
As a healer..I see mental illness not just as psychology but as energy that,s stagnant, blocked, suffocated energy.

Stigma is an energetic blockage, clogs the flow of life force, prana, Qi (chi). It keeps people trapped in the dark when all they need is a single candle.
And when honesty replaces shame, when someone finds the courage to speak, that candle is lit.
That is when the flow returns.
That is when healing begins.

But here is the deeper truth I wish someone had told me earlier…
When your prana or Qi is blocked, you may not always
express it outside but your body is already paying the price inside.
Every suppressed word, every buried emotion, every
moment of wallowing in low self-worth doesn't just
disappear..It settles.
It finds a place in your tissues, in your breath, in your very shape.

Suppressed emotions don't die.
They mutate..They become the fat on your body.
They become the illnesses in your bloodstream.

They become the chronic anxiety that sits on your chest.
They show up as comfort eating, as nights spent hiding in food instead of facing your pain.
They show up as isolation, not wanting to go out, not dressing up, dimming your own light because somewhere you've been made to believe you are unworthy of being seen.

For all the women, especially, these suppressed emotions find very specific places to live..
They turn into migraines that throb with every unspoken word.
They become thyroid imbalances from swallowing down truths you were never allowed to say.
They become hormonal issues, PCOD, infertility, as your creative energy is stifled instead of flowing freely.
They become digestive problems, IBS, ulcers, because you are constantly digesting everyone else's needs while starving your own.
They become autoimmune diseases, where your body turns against itself mirroring the way your spirit was constantly turned down by those around you.
They become hypertension, high cholesterol, diabetes, the body screaming for balance after years of emotional imbalance.

Not to scare you but only to make you aware of the
Stigma > suppression > disease chain very clear.

And all of this happens while she the woman, the wife, the mother, the genuine friend.. is holding everyone else's world together.

She takes care of the house.
She takes care of the children.
She takes care of your parents.
She takes care of your office colleagues.
She takes care of those corporate dinners, entertaining your guests, smiling at the right time, keeping everything afloat.

And she does it all without a word.. Without a demand.
In the quiet hope that one day she will be appreciated.

But instead of appreciation, she is met with dismissal.
Instead of acknowledgment, she is met with condescension.

Every time she tries to finish a sentence, she is cut.
Every time she dares to give an opinion, she is shut.
"Keep quiet. You don't know anything. You don't have brains. You just stay at home."
That is how narcissistic control works… it rewires your identity to nothingness, it reduces your entire being to
silence, while your body bares the cost.

G³ Goonj ~

The truth !
Mental illness is not madness.. Silence is madness.
Mental health care is not weakness..
Suppression is weakness.

So when the world whispers..
"Don't tell anyone, just stay strong"
I say this to you with all the authority of my scars and my healing..

Speak.. Heal..
Break that silent stigma..!!
Because your mind, your heart, your soul deserves to breathe free.

This is why I say…stigma is not just a social issue.
It is not just "mental health."
It is a whole-body disease, a whole-life disease, one that is born inside the soul and spreads into the body until you are no longer the woman you once were.

The outcome of suppression is this..
You no longer look like you.

You no longer live like you.
You become a stranger inside your own skin shaped not by your soul's desires but by the weight of every
silenced feeling.

Healing begins only when that cycle breaks.
When you stop apologising for your voice.
When you stop carrying the weight of everyone else's expectations. When you finally allow the blocked Qi to move, to flow, to breathe..
And.. with that.. everything starts to move along.

CHAPTER 9

SHOWDOWN WITH MENTAL RUMINATION

~THE SILENT ENEMY IN MY HEAD

Mental rumination is not loud. It does not storm into your life like grief or betrayal.
It seeps in.
Like a leaky tap dripping into a bucket you didn't even know was under the sink, filling slowly until one day it overflows.

I remember days where I sat for hours, circling the same thought like a moth circling a flame.
What will people say if I step out..?
What if I fail..?
What if I embarrass my family..?

The irony of rumination is that it convinces you that sitting still, obeying the "safer" rules of society, will protect you. But in truth, it drains you more than any mistake could ever do.

Now the Draining Cycle..

The Orthodox Cage
It begins in the house. The longer you sit inside, the more you start believing the voices of others are wiser than your own. You trade your raw instincts for second hand instructions.
"Don't dream too big."
"This is what girls in our family do."
"Stay within the four walls."

And without realising, you confuse safety with stagnation.

The Loop of Helplessness
Then comes the endless loop every decision becomes a debate, every dream becomes a burden. You are replaying the same conversations in your mind but never writing your own. Mental energy is consumed by "what ifs," leaving you exhausted without ever lifting a finger.

The Identity Leak
Rumination doesn't just waste time..it leaks your identity. The longer you sit in it, the more your skills, your gifts, your unique genius go unexplored. Like a book left unread on a shelf, your life gathers dust.

The Invisible Drain
This is where the damage becomes dangerous. Your body is sitting in one room, but your mind is trapped in cycles. You can sleep 12 hours and wake up more tired than someone who worked 12 hours.
Because rumination is not rest..
It's silent theft.

What I later understood is this..
Rumination is not a flaw of the mind, it is a frightened protector. It loops not because it is weak but because it is trying to keep you from risk, judgment and loss. The mind was trained in homes where obedience was praised more than courage, where approval felt safer than authenticity.
So it learned to pause life rather than live it. But protection that outlives its purpose becomes a prison. And the moment I stopped asking my mind for permission and started listening to my body, my calling, and my silence…rumination loosened its grip. Not because fear vanished, but because courage finally outranked it.

Kailash: The Mirror That Broke the Cycle

If I had listened to those rumination's, I would have happily walked away from even taking the step toward the Kailash pilgrimage. My family was against me traveling in the condition I was…with an injured back, strapped with supports just to get through the journey. My GuruMa's dream that we die in a landslide..

And if I had stayed back, I would have lost the greatest opportunity of my life, to be in that storm, to see the universe at its peak in the hustling fury of Brahmaputra river, in that unstoppable rain and in those seventeen days of zero sunlight, with landslides all the way throughout, massive traffic jams, standing at the edge of the ghats not knowing whether the bus tire would slip through the muck into the valley or whether your first step down the bus would make you slide into that abyss and end your journey right there.

From landslides and endless traffic jamming our path to even reach or experience Kailash…it was all worth it.
Or I would have missed the universe's beauty at its rawest, its wildest, its best.

Something inside me fought.
I fought through those circling thoughts. I sat in silence. Instead of entertaining the fears that were pounding my heart and mind, I put my foot down or perhaps, more truthfully, there was a divine grace that summoned me there, that grace insisted I be present, that refused to let me shrink away.

And so I found myself on this pilgrimage with an injured back, strapped with belts and gears to hold me together through every jolting bus ride. Every hurdle the bus jumped brought tears to my eyes but still, I kept moving through all those struggles, through those innumerable moments, And yes it was all worth it..

Because once abundance starts flowing, it doesn't limit itself to money. It comes as the abundance of peace. The abundance of energy. And the abundance of calling..
A calling that rings with such clarity,
it rewires your entire being..!

Kailash showed me that night that storms are not punishments but revelations. The mountain doesn't test you to break you...
it tests you to free you..!

Breaking Out of the Cycle
The first time I dared to step out to take my wisdom seriously, to explore my own skills, I felt the rust falling off my spirit.

The same way I stepped into Kailash storms and found serenity on the other side, I realised life outside rumination is wild but beautiful.
When you act, doors open..
Financial energy shows up..Collaborations appear..Vitality returns.

Abundance doesn't visit the one who waits. It runs to the one who moves.

G^3 Goonj~

Rumination is nothing but a graveyard of "almosts."
Almost spoken.!
Almost tried.!!
Almost lived.!!!

Kailash reminded me that storms are not proof of weakness but invitations to strength. The mountain does not reward the one who trek the most..It rewards the one who dares to step out of the cycle and into surrender.

If you are reading this, ask yourself…
are you circling the same thought or are you stepping into your sacred storm..?

Because beyond rumination lies a river of abundance…financial, creative, spiritual…flowing and waiting for you..

CHAPTER 10

SHOWDOWN WITH EMOTIONAL FANATICS

~ANATOMY OF EMOTIONAL FANATICISM

There are storms that rage outside the body and then there are storms that live inside human hearts.
Louder.. Wilder.. More consuming.

Emotional fanatics are not people who simply feel deeply. They worship their emotions.. They kneel before them.. They surrender their sovereignty to them.

For them emotion is not a current to pass through.
It becomes.. a weapon.. An idol.. A prison..!

They declare wars in the name of love.
They light fires in the name of anger.
They drown entire relationships in the name of attachment.

Their feelings are not companions.
They are dictators.

Their moods are not weather.
They are climate.

And if you have ever fallen into their orbit you know this truth.
You do not merely meet them.
You are dragged....Whipped, Scorched by their intensity.

Over years of working with people I began to recognise patterns inside these storms. Emotional fanaticism wears many masks yet the core remains the same. The emotion is no longer experienced. It is obeyed.

Some are **Worshippers of Pain**, cling to grief as if it were sacred scripture. Every wound is displayed like a medal. Healing feels like betrayal to their suffering.

Some are **Zealots of Love**, confuse obsession with devotion. They call it love while quietly locking the beloved
inside invisible bars.

Some **Rage Disciples**, treat rage as righteousness. A spark is enough. Destruction becomes proof of courage.

Few of them are **Hope Addicts**, overdose on hope. They reject reality and shame anyone who questions their blind optimism.

Some are **Victim Preachers,** preach victimhood like a
sermon. Sympathy becomes their fuel. Accountability
remains untouched.

Different faces.. Same hunger..!

I remember being pulled into one such storm.
Someone's grief became my leash. I was not allowed to laugh because they were hurting. I was not allowed to heal
because they had not. I was not allowed to move because their feet were stuck.
At first I called this compassion.

Later I understood it was fanaticism.

They were not asking for empathy. They were demanding worship of their pain. And I was bowing.

That moment was my wake-up call.

When Healing Turned Into a Loop..
There was a client who came to me for years.

Every session unfolded the same story.
The same heartbreak..The same betrayals..The same tears..

So often repeated that the pain had carved grooves into her nervous system.

Initially I believed this was depth. Healing does ask us to return again and again. But something was wrong. The
needle never moved. We were not peeling layers. We were circling.

And slowly guilt crept into my own body.
She was investing her time.. Her energy.. Her money..
And nothing was shifting.

I questioned myself relentlessly.
What kind of healer allows someone to remain frozen for years.
I carried that weight like a stone in my chest.

During my sadhana the answer struck me with unsettling clarity.
She was not failing.
I was not failing..
This was not stagnation..

This was choice.
She was choosing the loop.. She was surviving on it.
She was not a victim of her emotions..
She was a fanatic of them..

Her pain had become nourishment.
Her tears had become oxygen.
Her emotional eruptions were the only moments she felt alive.

The storm was not drowning her.. It was sustaining her.
Healing was not freedom to her.. It was a threat.

Because without the wound she would lose the only anchor she trusted. Her suffering..!

Some people do not come to release. They come to protect their wounds. They build altars around them and ask you to kneel alongside.

Then there was **Resistance..**
Whenever I suggested something different the resistance surfaced immediately.

Silence..Meditation..Breath..Energy work..

Her eyes would harden. Her voice would sharpen.
She accused me of not listening because she had not finished narrating her pain.

The wound had become her mirror.
She no longer recognised herself without it.
I could feel the element imbalance clearly.
Her **water element** overflowed. Emotion flooded everything.
Her inner **fire** had dimmed. There was no spark left to ignite transformation.

Each time I tried to stoke that fire she dragged me back into the flood.

I went into my own sadhana again and again asking for clarity to help her rise above this emotional trap..
The answer arrived softly.

She was trapped in Emotional Fanaticism.

In early stages it can soften..
With discipline.. With willingness.. With awareness..
But when identity merges with the wound.. the grip
becomes fierce. It drains the one trapped inside it and it drains the healer who steps too close.

Then came the layer of Fantasy Inside the Loop
What took me many sessions to unravel this.
She was not addicted to pain itself.
She was addicted to the fantasy stitched inside it.

The illusion that if she held the emotion tightly enough the past might return.
The lost person might come back.
The broken relationship might repair itself.
The missed moment that she clanged tightly on to..might replay.

She was not living in the present. She lived in a private dreamscape where emotion promised control over time and destiny.

To leave that fantasy would mean waking up to reality. A place where what was lost would not return.
So she stayed.... Looping.. Wallowing
Praying to pain like it was a God..

Not because she refused healing.
Because she believed emotion was power.

My Showdown

And the part I didn't want to admit for a long time now..
I wasn't only witnessing that loop in the people who came to me.
I had lived it..
My version wasn't loud or reckless. It didn't announce itself. It lived quietly in emotion. I stayed inside my pain longer than truth ever asked me to. I replayed old wounds until they became familiar enough to feel like home.
I mistook intensity for honesty and suffering for depth, convincing myself that staying close to the ache meant I was being real.
There were phases where being hurt became part of my identity, where telling the story again felt like release when it was really

just another hit. Even my wakeful nights once felt sacred, until I saw clearly that my nervous system wasn't listening anymore…it was buzzing.

Even fear carried its own chemistry.
The edge..The charge..
The strange sense of being alive inside discomfort.
I wasn't healing then, even though I was calling it self-work. I was stimulating myself through emotion and quietly
feeding the same loop I believed I was rising above.

The shift didn't come through insight or explanation or even help at first. It came the moment I stopped feeding it.

As a energy healer, this was the hardest truth to sit with…that I didn't need to fix the pain, heal it or turn it into meaning.
I needed to stop rehearsing it. I stopped narrating it. I stopped asking it…to prove something about me.
I let the emotion exist without letting it decide who I was.
That was the interruption..Not suppression..Not bypassing..

Just the refusal to keep living inside repetition. When pain is felt without commentary, without performance, without identity wrapped around it, the nervous system finally stands down. The body no longer has to stay alert. The mind stops circling the same ground.
You don't step out of the loop by fighting it or understanding it better. You step out by ending the role you play inside it.
I learned to feel fully and then leave. And in that quiet refusal to keep circling, something steadier than intensity took over. The charge dissolved.. The grip loosened..
And finally the loop collapsed.

I share this only so you know you are safe here because I understand this place not as a guide but as someone who once stood exactly where you are..!

The Cost of this Storm..
Emotional fanaticism consumes everything it touches.
It burns bridges because fire feels justified.
It drains others because tears feel sacred.
It imprisons souls because attachment is mistaken for love.
It rewrites truth because feelings feel like facts.

The most dangerous illusion is this.
Intensity is mistaken for depth and wisdom quietly disappears.

Now the **Antidote** to this..
You do not outshout an emotional fanatic.
You do not outweep them.
You do not outlove them.

You become still.
You become the mountain in their storm.

Silence and steadiness are not passive tools.
They are fierce.. They are protective.. They are sovereign..

Emotional fanatics feed on reaction.
Attention fuels the loop..Resistance feeds it..Pity sustains it.
The moment you react you enter their orbit.

When you stay grounded while they rage. When you breathe while they flood. When you remain clear while they spiral. The cycle weakens.
This is not abandonment..It is refusal to worship the wound.

You say without words
I see you..I hear you..
But I will not bow to this emotion.

For healers this stillness is protection.. For seekers it is possibility.

Not because it forces change.
Because it introduces a quiet discomfort.
A new mirror.. A different way of being.

This medicine does not do more.
It is more..!
More rooted..,More present..More unshakeable.

And when everything else fails this becomes the most radical intervention of all.
You remind them gently but firmly that emotions are teachers not tyrants.

And you remember for yourself.
Compassion is not captivity..Empathy is not enslavement.

G³ Goonj~

If you are entangled with an emotional fanatic ask yourself honestly.

Am I supporting healing or feeding addiction to pain..?
Am I loving or enabling..?
Am I staying from compassion or from fear of guilt, wrath or abandonment..?

Fanaticism always blinds.
Emotional fanaticism seduces because it disguises itself as love, care and righteousness.

You are allowed to step back and say
I honour your storm.
But I will not drown with you.

Here is the truth I leave you with..
If you see yourself anywhere in these pages, know this..
There is nothing wrong with you..

Loops form when we are left to figure things out alone for too long. I know that place..
I needed someone to point the way and there was no one, so I stayed tangled longer than I should have.

Today, it doesn't have to be that way.
Asking for help is no longer a weakness or a dramatic moment. It's as ordinary as picking up a phone and dialing a number.
You don't need a hardened shell to survive this and you don't need to dissolve into it either.
It's okay to be caught in an emotional loop but make sure its not permanent.
Don't get comfortable there.

If this chapter feels familiar, if you recognise yourself standing in this light…
Remember…that you can change what comes next.
Reach out.. Share.. Take the step..

You don't have to walk this part alone…sometimes a simple guidance is enough to shift the perspective you've been stuck in.

CHAPTER 11

SHOWDOWN WITH THE DOPAMINE FACTOR

~THE ILLUSION OF THE HIGH

I didn't understand dopamine when I first met it.
I only knew the feeling.

That sudden clarity when the mind sharpens without effort.
That internal hum where the body feels ready before you ask it to move.
That sense of being switched-on, while the rest of the world feels half-asleep.

For a long time, I mistook that feeling for aliveness.

I saw it first in others before I could recognise it in myself. People who moved fast, spoke faster, lived as if slowing down would erase them. Their days were loud and packed. Their calendars overflowed. Their nights never really ended; they only dimmed. Even rest had to be earned, justified, scheduled.

One man I knew lived entirely in acceleration. His mornings began with stimulants strong enough to jolt him awake before his eyes fully opened. His phone was already alive before his body was. Conversations overlapped. Plans stacked on plans. Laughter came easily and vanished just as quickly. When he sat still, even for a minute, something in him twitched.

Once, almost defensively, he said, "If I stop, everything will catch up."

He thought he meant failure.
What he really meant was emptiness.

At the time, I didn't have language for what I was witnessing. I only noticed that nothing ever landed inside him. Joy passed through..Stress passed through..People passed through. Even pleasure never stayed long enough to settle. His eyes were always searching, as if waiting for the next signal.

I saw the crash long before he did.

What I didn't realise then was that dopamine wasn't just driving his life. It was shaping his identity.

Dopamine doesn't only reward pleasure.
It rewards anticipation..It rewards pursuit..
It rewards intensity..

And this is where things quietly turn.

Because once the brain learns that intensity equals reward, it stops caring where that intensity comes from.
Joy or pain.. Success or struggle..
The chemistry is the same.
The story changes but the nervous system doesn't argue.

This is the part most people miss.

You don't need happiness to trigger dopamine.
You only need charge.
That charge can come from achievement or conflict.
From urgency or validation.
From being needed or being wounded.
Even suffering.. especially suffering that feels meaningful, can become a reliable source.

I didn't learn this from books.
I learned it much later by watching myself.

Another phase in my life, when struggle became my fuel. I didn't call it that at the time.
I called it strength.. I called it resilience.. I called it depth..
But beneath those respectable words was something more chemical and more dangerous.

I noticed how alive I felt when things were intense. When emotions ran high.
When problems demanded my full
attention.
When I was pulled into complexity.
My system responded to chaos like it was purpose.

Calm felt suspicious..Ease felt unearned..Stillness felt like absence.
And pain, strangely, felt familiar enough to feel safe.

That was the moment something unsettling became clear: even suffering can turn into a dopamine loop.
Not because pain feels good but because it gives the brain a reason to stay alert.
It gives identity a role.. It gives life a storyline.. It creates meaning where silence would otherwise appear.

The mind doesn't always chase pleasure.
Sometimes it chases relevance.
And relevance is intoxicating.

This is where dopamine becomes tricky. Not only in
obvious addictions but in the subtle ways we organise our lives around stimulation.
Emotional stimulation..Cognitive stimulation..Moral stimulation..Even spiritual stimulation.

I've seen people addicted to outrage.

To being right.
To being needed.
To being wounded.

I've seen pain worn like proof of depth. Trauma repeated like a credential. Stories rehearsed until the charge fades and the retelling has to sharpen just to land the same effect.

The nervous system doesn't distinguish between noble struggle and compulsive struggle.
It only knows repetition and reward.

This is why some people resist healing even when healing is available. Because healing threatens the very chemistry that has been holding their sense of self together.

When pain goes quiet, dopamine drops.
When intensity fades, the system panics.
When peace arrives, the brain doesn't recognise itself.
This isn't weakness.. It's pure conditioning..

Dopamine is not a pleasure chemical in the simplistic sense. It's a motivation chemical.
It tells the brain..
What matters.. What to repeat.. What to move toward..
Over time, it becomes a sculptor of personality.

That's why the same chemistry can build focus or fracture sanity.
Why it can sharpen intelligence or dissolve it.
Why it can turn ambition into obsession and devotion into dependency.

The difference is never the chemical.
The difference is awareness.

Just exactly when I had to face my own patterns honestly. Not dramatically.. Not spiritually.. Just truthfully..

I noticed how quickly my system reached for stimulation when things slowed down. How easily urgency replaced presence. How often my worth felt tied to momentum.

Even spiritual practices weren't immune. Depth became another high. Insight another hit. Transformation another chase.

That was my real showdown.
Not with pleasure..Not with addiction..
But with the part of me that equated intensity with meaning.

I had to ask a quieter question:
who am I when nothing is firing..?

That question terrified my nervous system.

Because without the spikes, without urgency, without emotional charge, there was a flatness I didn't know how to inhabit. A blankness that felt like disappearance.

This is where most people turn back. They return to noise. To productivity.. To drama.. To pain..
To anything that restores the familiar chemical hum.

I stayed..

Not heroically.. Not gracefully.. I stayed because something deeper was tired of the loop.
And in that staying, something shifted.
There is another chemistry beneath dopamine.
Slower, Quieter..More stable..

It doesn't spike..It doesn't shout..It doesn't perform..
But it holds.

When the nervous system begins to trust steadiness, dopamine stops needing to compensate. Motivation no longer needs urgency. Desire no longer needs desperation. Focus no longer needs pressure.

This shift doesn't come from control. It comes from re-education.
I didn't eliminate dopamine from my life.
I just stopped worshipping it.

I began to notice which actions created clean energy rather than charged energy. Which engagements left me full rather than wired. Which conversations deepened rather than stimulated.

Moving without pushing..Working without racing.
Connecting without performing.
Practicing without chasing experience.

And slowly, something rewired.

The highs softened..The crashes shortened..
The space between desire and action widened enough for choice to exist.

This is where dopamine becomes an ally again.
A compass rather than a dictator.

Not every pull needs to be followed.
Not every urge needs obedience.
Not every intensity needs amplification.

Some sensations are invitations to pause rather than pursue.

I wish more people understood this..
You are not broken because you crave intensity.
You are conditioned.
And conditioning can be unwound.

Often, beneath the chase is not greed but fear.
Fear of silence..Fear of insignificance..Fear of rest..

The system learned that movement equals safety. That stimulation equals survival.

Once that belief loosens, dopamine stops hijacking identity.

It becomes what it was meant to be
a messenger, not a master..!

I no longer measure my life by how alive I feel in moments of intensity. I measure it by how present I remain when nothing dramatic is happening.

That is a different kind of aliveness.
Quieter.. Deeper..Sustainable.

G³ Goonj~

There was a time when I believed desire was truth. If I wanted something strongly enough, I followed it.
Coffee..Conversation..Work..Connection..Even pain.
I thought impulse was intuition. It took me years to see the difference.

Discipline didn't cage me.
It freed me from being dragged by every internal signal.
Once I began observing rather than reacting, patterns revealed themselves. My moods weren't mysterious. They were predictable. Linked to habits I defended. When I changed the inputs, the weather inside me changed too.

I no longer chase spikes. I choose steadiness. Not because it's boring but because it's honest. The nervous system relaxes when it knows it doesn't have to perform to be worthy of rest.

Night became sacred again. Not as recovery from exhaustion, but as a return to myself. When the brain is allowed to downshift without negotiation, it remembers how to repair.

At first, I thought night was my natural rhythm.

Later, I realised it wasn't night I was loyal to.. it was the absence of demand.

That distinction changed everything.

If quiet alone could make me feel alive, then dopamine wasn't responding to darkness or creativity or rebellion against sleep. It was responding to regulation.

Night had simply removed the noise for me.
It had done the regulating on my behalf.

That meant the chemistry I was tasting wasn't rare or mysterious.. It was just unfamiliar.

The question then became uncomfortable and unavoidable. What would happen if my nervous system didn't have to wait for the world to sleep in order to feel safe..?
And then one day, without drama, my chemistry changed.
There came a phase where discipline stopped feeling like effort.
I didn't force it..I didn't chase it..It arrived quietly.

One fine day I started waking up early without resistance. Sleeping earlier without bargaining. Eating when hungry, not when restless. Moving without pushing.

I noticed it only in hindsight.

My days felt steady. My thoughts clearer.
My body cooperative in a way it had never been before.

And then it struck me…This was dopamine too.

But it didn't spike..It didn't demand.
It didn't borrow energy from tomorrow.
It held.

I had felt dopamine rushes before sharp, bright, demanding. They always came with urgency and always asked for more..This didn't.

There was aliveness, yes but without hunger.
Focus without pressure. Presence without negotiation.

For the first time, I didn't feel the need to repeat the experience.

That's when I understood what had changed.

Earlier, dopamine came from extraction.
Through stimulation..Through intensity..Through pushing the system to respond.

This was different chemistry altogether.

Not appetite…Alignment…

Once I tasted this, every old high revealed itself as imitation.

The nights I waited for.
The urgency I defended.
The rushes I thought were happiness.

They weren't wrong..They were just immature.

This steady, unremarkable, deeply alive state.. this was my real dopamine factor.

Dopamine is not the enemy.
It is a signal.

But signals are meant to be read, not obeyed blindly.

I had to learn that not every pull was pointing forward. Some were pointing inward. Some were pointing to wounds disguised as wants.

The illusion of the high is not pleasure.
It is the belief that intensity equals meaning.
When that belief dissolved, something steadier took its place.

Not numbness..Not detachment..
But a grounded hum that doesn't need fireworks to exist.

That is the north I follow now..!

CHAPTER 12

SHOWDOWN WITH THE OVERDRIVE

~IT'S NOT INSOMNIA..IT'S SANCTUARY

A powerful turning point in the chapter is where overdrive shifts from survival… to sacred self-connection.

For every woman who became the engine, the oil, the wheels and the road. Please accept my sincere gratitude.

The Clock Was Never My Friend..
I don't remember when I started living on borrowed hours.
Maybe it was when I first became a mother or maybe even before that
When being a daughter meant anticipating what my parents needed before they said it.
When being a wife meant dissolving my needs to keep peace.
When being a daughter-in-law meant smiling even when the blood in my feet froze from fatigue.

But one thing I know for sure
Somewhere along the way,
I became the woman who stretched 24 hours into 30.
Not just once but every single day.

While most women wind down by midnight,
I began **another shift**..
From 12 a.m. to 5 a.m..
I'd be wide awake..

Cleaning..Fixing..Planning..Comforting..Managing..
Sometimes holding back tears.
Sometimes not even aware that I had any left.
Because my body was functioning,
And that meant..I was fine, right..?

Wrong..!
I wasn't fine..I was in **overdrive**.
And I was alone in it.

When 'She Can Handle It' Became a Curse..
They called me a perfectionist.
They said it like a compliment.
"Oh she's so particular… she likes to do it all herself."
"No no… don't help her…she doesn't like it."
"She'll shout if you enter the kitchen. She's too intense."

You know what's worse than being unseen..?
Being misunderstood in plain sight..!
I didn't do everything because I wanted control.
I did everything because no one else would.
Because I didn't trust your temporary help.
Because every time I asked, I was met with delays, rolled eyes, half-done jobs or happy yes's without any action for hours…

Don't romanticise my burnout by calling it efficiency.
Don't make my exhaustion a character trait.
Don't label my need for order as a flaw.

Because guess what..
You were just watching and I was bleeding in silence.

Then Came the Pets… and the Lies of 'Support'
You brought them in because they were cute.
Not one.. Not two.. But four..
With sparkling eyes and wagging tails.
With responsibilities you never shouldered.

You played for five minutes and I cleaned up for hours.
Of course I had help.. but they were on a clock too and not 24 hr at service..
And pets need to go when they need to go..

You posted their pictures, claiming ..My Pets !
And I woke up at 3 a.m. to clean their mess, calm their anxiety, take them to the vet, feed them, groom them, above all toilet training that never fell in place, still smile at the chaos.

I didn't mind loving them.
Though I had a choice, given my allergies..
But I never agreed to raise them alone.
I had enough beating hearts to care for.

But you added more…
And walked away from them when the charm faded or you had another distraction.
Leaving me with another layer of motherhood I never signed up for.

Exhaustion kept piling and the Night Became My Only Escape..
With all the noise, all the duties, all the "Can you just…?" of the day..
I realised there was no time left for me.
No time for my mind to unwind, for my creativity to
surface..
For my body to breathe, to rushed or required.
So I started staying up… just an hour at first.
Then two.
Then the whole night..

And before I knew it,
I was nocturnal..!
And for my GuruMa, nishachari..!

She's the only one who accepted me as I was..
When someone questioned my pattern…She had a perfect answer for them..
Even if she wakes up late she can finish in a couple of hours what you take 8 hours to finish. So concentrate on your lives.

At first, they mocked it.
"Oh, she doesn't sleep!"
"Why are you up all night? Must be watching nonsense."
But they didn't know
That night was my therapy.. My prayer..My rebellion.. and eventually **My salvation..!**

Because when the world sleeps, It stops needing me.
That's when I finally get to need myself.
At night, I get to listen to music I love.
To write without interruption.
To watch something without guilt.
To take care of my skin, my hair, my aching body.
To speak to God.
Do my Sadhana.
To feel like I exist beyond my usefulness.

So yes, I became nocturnal.
And no, I'm not sorry.
That's the only time the world stops owning me
And I start remembering who I am.

Then came repercussions as I was on a overdrive…

What Happens to a Woman in Overdrive?
Here's what happens..
-Her back hurts from unexpressed rage.
-Her stomach churns with swallowed words.
-Her heart grows heavy with invisible bricks of thanklessness.

~ Her sleep disappears.
~ Her voice cracks, not from age but from years of silence.
~ Her brain forgets not because she's careless but because she's carrying.. too much.
Her instant defence.. NO.. to anything new or anything that can take some more time from her that she couldn't afford.
And when she finally breaks, You call her moody.
Overreacting..Too sensitive..Hormonal..!!!

Ohh don't you dare ..?

You who didn't lift a finger,
You who thought speaking was contribution enough,
You who judged while I carried your weight.. Nope!

To All Who Took Me for Granted..
This is not a sob story..This is my showdown..!

I am not asking for your pity.
I am asking for your awareness
I am demanding your respect.
Don't put me on a pedestal and then leave me up there..
Alone..! Cold..! Expected to perform perfection while everyone watches from below.

You sit all day working or doing things that interest you and for me most I do.. because I must.
So Do not tag me as "the one who never needs help"
Because I do…Desperately..!

Sometimes, all I want is for someone to say:
"Sit. I've got this."
And actually mean it.. do it my way my obsessive way as you've watched me all years you've been around

A Woman Is Not a Machine.

Even If She Behaves Like One.

The truth is..I'm not superhuman.
I'm not your unpaid therapist, chef, cleaner, planner and babysitter, pet sitter..
I'm not a perfectly oiled machine built to run on sacrifice and fumes.
I am human.. A woman..
And I've run in overdrive for way too long.

So now, if my pause pinches you
Don't ask me "What's wrong?"
If you're genuinely concerned..
Ask yourself
☟
"What have we been doing wrong… for her to reach this point..?"

And to every woman like me,
Burning from both ends..I see you..I am you.
And this is your permission slip
To rest..To say no..
To fall apart without apology.
To stop before your body forces you to.

Because your worth is not in your output.
It's in your being.. in the moment

And if that means staying up while the world sleeps
just to finally feel like yourself…then may the night always embrace you…like a mother, no one else remembered to be for you.

I pray & wish for your
Survival to self- connection… swish.!

G^3 Goonj~

This is our song…

Tonight put the armour down,
heels by the door, crown still on.
I've been holding the ceiling up somehow,
even when no one's around.

I need the rest..
I'm done with the test.
You see my tired eyes,
do I need to justify?

Let the world wait outside,
I don't owe the dark my light.
I don't need a fix or a hand,
I just need somewhere safe to land.

I've held the fire way too long,
you can hear the ache in my song.
You keep the world warm tonight,
I've burned past my own light.

No more living in yesterdays
I carried the weight that never paid,
I walked away, I choose my space
I'm here, I'm real, Let it stay this way.

I'm humble, I'm kind,
Just a tired rebel still trying.
Call me weak if I need to breathe,
I've been strong beyond belief.

I don't disappear, I don't fall,
I just stop carrying it all.
If everything cracks when I rest,
then it leaned too hard on my chest.

I've been the answer, the fix, the glue,
the calm that everyone runs to.
But even a heart needs quiet to live..
I've given enough.

So let the sink stay full tonight,
let the house look human in the light.
If love is real, it knows when to stay,
not only when I lead the way.

I'm standing still, I'm on my own,
easing what wrapped around my bones.
Not quitting, not losing ground,
just breathing now,
without a sound.

CHAPTER 13

SHOWDOWN WITH INSOMNIA

~WHEN THE WORLD SLEPT, I WAS SHOWN THE STARS.

This chapter is not about insomnia. It is about consciousness arriving when the world is unconscious.

For as long as I can remember, sleep was never my loyal companion. While the world folded itself neatly into night and surrendered to rest without resistance, I remained awake, alert, aware, moving through hours that most people passed through without memory.

Night after night, year after year..

I lived inside a rhythm that did not match the collective clock. My mind did not dim when the lights went out. My body did not collapse into unconsciousness just because the world expected it to. Instead, something inside me stayed switched on, attentive, observant, quietly alive.

I walked through long stretches of silence where thought did not race but deepened. I wandered inner corridors that did not frighten me but invited me. Somewhere along that long continuum of wakefulness, I turned fifty. And by then, it was undeniable that I had never truly slept more than a few hours a day in my entire adult life.

This baffled people. It worried them. It unsettled them in ways they could not always articulate. The questions came steadily, sometimes wrapped in concern, sometimes edged with accusation.
How do you live like this..?
Why are you awake when everyone else sleeps..?
Is it anxiety or pain or something unresolved..?
Is it exhaustion disguised as strength or madness disguised as spirituality..?
Even within my own home, my nights became a topic of discussion and discomfort. At times it was whispered as worry. At times it was hurled as frustration. My wakefulness made others uneasy because it could not be easily explained, corrected or controlled.

What they never understood was this… my nights were not empty. They were not haunted. They were not hollow. They were full.
Full of searching, full of inquiry, full of sacred solitude.
I was not lying awake replaying fears or rehearsing pain.
I was not wrestling with panic or drowning in unprocessed trauma. I was alive at night in a way that felt natural to me, even if it felt unnatural to everyone else. Those hours were not something I endured. They were something I inhabited.

Let me be very clear here, because this distinction matters. This was not sleeplessness born from careless panic or nervous collapse. This was not a body in danger. This was a body in alert reverence. There is a kind of insomnia that fractures the mind, drains the nervous system and leaves a person depleted and afraid. And then there is a kind that sharpens awareness, heightens perception and creates an unusual intimacy with silence. I was not running from sleep. Sleep simply stepped aside so something else could arrive. My wakefulness did not feel like a malfunction. It felt like a different mode of being that I did not yet know how to name.

In those quiet hours, I watched films that moved something inside me, some for entertainment but mostly for resonance.
I read without distraction.
I wrote without agenda.
I danced without witnesses.
I created without deadlines.
I meditated without discipline.
I reflected without censorship.
I soaked in whatever spoke to my soul without needing to justify why it mattered. What began as a strange habit of staying awake when others slept slowly shaped itself into a pattern, then a rhythm, then a way of life.
For many years, I told myself it was just a stubborn quirk. Something odd about me. Something inconvenient. Something I might one day fix.

I tried to interpret myself the way the world did. Maybe I was different in the wrong way. Maybe I was broken in a quiet place no one could see. A DNA link interrupted or Maybe I was simply made wrong. These thoughts did not torment me but they hovered. They followed me into daylight where my body finally allowed itself to rest.

Yes, I missed many things. I missed lunches that unfolded easily in the middle of the day. I missed early morning gatherings and social rituals that assumed everyone shared the same biological timing. I missed celebrations that took place when my system was finally shutting down.

Because those hours when the world was awake were often the only hours my body allowed itself to recover. While others laughed over brunch or sipped coffee in crowded circles, I was asleep, not from laziness or withdrawal but from deep recovery. Not just physical recovery but spiritual restoration.

For a long time, I felt bad about missing out. I carried a low grade guilt that suggested I was somehow failing at participation. Until one day I realised that I was not missing anything that was meant for me. Many of those rooms were filled with noise rather than meaning, with gossip rather than connection, with shallow conversations and quiet judgments that travelled faster than compassion.
Often, the same people who worried about my nights had plenty to say about me when I was not present.

What I had instead was stillness.
Not emptiness.. Stillness..
A charismatic aura that made people, magnetically pulled towards me.
A gorgeous, beautiful silence that did not demand performance.
A sanctuary no one else could see and no one else could enter unless invited.
Somewhere around a decade ago, the fog began to lift.
Not suddenly.. Not dramatically.. Quietly.. Gradually..

I realised that I was not made wrong. I was made different. And difference does not always need correction. Sometimes it needs understanding.

While most people were trapped in mechanical loops of living alarms, deadlines, obligations repeated until they lost meaning.. I had been given a strange freedom disguised as inconvenience. My nights were not an accident. They were not a punishment. They were not a defect. This was never about restlessness. It was about remembrance.
It was an invitation from the universe to meet myself without interruption.

My Showdown

The hours between three in the morning and five in the morning are unlike any other hours on this earth. I had spent most of my life awake during this window long before I knew it had a name. Ancient wisdom calls it Brahma Muhurat. I did not learn this from books first. I recognised it in my body. These hours carry a quality that is difficult to describe to someone who has never been there consciously. The mind is naturally quieter.
The emotional noise of the world has not yet restarted.
The boundary between the inner and the unseen feels thinner. Thought becomes less aggressive. Insight arrives without force. Creativity flows without self correction and prayers feels less like asking and more like listening. The soul seems to clean itself of residue accumulated during the day.

These were the hours when truth whispered.
Not loudly.. Not theatrically.. Softly and unmistakably..
What many people mistook for insomnia was often overdrive, not in the sense of speed but in the sense of sensitivity. A nervous system tuned too finely to shut down blindly. A consciousness that stayed receptive when others went offline. My body was not exhausted. It was vigilant. My mind was not restless. It was receiving.

Through sleepless nights, I did not break down. I broke open. Through long stretches of silence, I discovered a voice inside me that was not reactive, not anxious, not defensive. A voice that did not speak in sentences but in knowing.
Insomnia was not my enemy. It was my initiation. A doorway that did not announce itself as sacred at first. A portal that opened me slowly to deeper layers of life, spirit and self.

That said, this must be stated clearly. Not all insomnia is sacred. And not all sleeplessness carries a message. When wakefulness comes with fear, collapse or depletion, it asks for care and support.

It asks for gentleness and intervention. But when it comes with clarity instead of chaos, with curiosity instead of panic, with awareness instead of dread, it deserves to be listened to rather than fought.

Over time, I learned to honour these hours instead of resisting them. I stopped trying to force myself into someone else's rhythm. I prepared for wakefulness the way others prepared for sleep. A dim light. A pot of warm jasmine tea. A notebook close by. A breath that said to my own body.. if I am awake, let it be sacred.

Today, I no longer resent my sleep patterns. I revere them. They were designed this way. They protected me from spaces I did not belong to. They kept me awake while the world numbed itself. They tuned my body and soul to frequencies most people never pause long enough to hear.

So no, this was never just about sleep. It was about soul timing. It was the universe's wild hidden blessing. It was how the Divine chose to keep me awake, not just at night but in life..
What looked like isolation transformed into insight.
What felt like restlessness revealed purpose. The universe had heard my strength long before I had the language to name it.

G^3 Goonj~

Now to you my dear reader…If you have ever felt different, if your rhythms do not match the world's expectations, if your body refuses their clocks and your mind wakes up precisely when everything else dulls itself, there is nothing wrong with you. Some people are built to blend. Some are built to listen. Some lives unfold in daylight. Some are shaped in the hours no one else wants to touch.

What looks like misalignment is often deeper calibration. What feels like isolation is sometimes protection. What appears as restlessness may be awareness that has nowhere to land yet. I spent years believing I needed to fix myself, to correct my rhythm, to apologise for how I functioned. But clarity does not arrive through effort. It arrives when the noise recedes enough to hear what has always been there.

I was never meant to sleep through certain hours. I was meant to stand watch. To notice what others miss. To receive before I could explain. And if something in you recognises this without needing proof, trust that recognition. Not everything meaningful arrives with permission. Not everything sacred comes wrapped as comfort.

This chapter was never about insomnia. It is about consciousness arriving when the world is unconscious.
For anyone who has ever felt this truth but lacked language…
it speaks beyond you without abandoning you.

CHAPTER 14

SHOWDOWN WITH THE CHRONICALLY LOQUACIOUS

~WHEN WORDS OVERFLOW AND MEANING EVAPORATES

There's a certain kind of silence that speaks volumes.
And then… there are volumes of words that say absolutely nothing.

Some conversations leave you lighter.
Others leave you tired in a way sleep cannot fix.

This chapter is about the second kind.

There is a kind of silence that nourishes. It restores. It gives shape to thought and space to breath. And then there is another experience altogether, one where silence never arrives because it is not allowed to. Where words keep pouring not to connect but to dominate the air. To occupy every inch of emotional territory. To leave no room for anyone else to exist fully.

This chapter is not about people who love language. I love language. I live inside words. This is about something else. It is about the chronic overflow of speech that erases meaning instead of creating it. About conversations that never become conversations. About listening that turns into endurance.

The chronically loquacious are not simply talkative. They are relentless. They speak as if silence is dangerous. As if a pause might expose something they cannot afford to feel. They speak to fill.. To secure.. To remain in control..
And often without realising it they leave others depleted long after the sound of their voice has faded.

If you have never been on the receiving end of this you might think this is a mild irritation. A personality quirk. Something solved with patience or humour. But those who have lived with it know better. They know the specific fatigue that comes from being talked at instead of spoken with. The exhaustion that does not come from noise alone but from invisibility.

There is a moment that always arrives in these encounters. It is the moment when you realise you have not been asked a single question. Not one. Your presence has not been registered beyond its usefulness as an audience.
You are nodding..You are smiling..You are offering cues..
that in healthy dialogue would invite exchange.
But here they change nothing…he stream continues uninterrupted.

What drains you is not just the length of the talking. It is the absence of reciprocity. The absence of curiosity. The subtle message that your interior life does not matter enough to be explored.

This is where emotional fatigue begins.

Chronic loquacity is invasive. It colonises mental space.
It leaves the listener carrying fragments of someone else's unprocessed thoughts long after the interaction ends. You walk away heavier than you arrived. Not because anything meaningful was shared but because your nervous system was forced to hold more than it consented to.

What many do not understand is that excessive talking is rarely about communication. It is about regulation.
It is how some people manage anxiety or insecurity.
They face a terror of being irrelevant.
Words become armour. Noise becomes protection. If the mouth stays busy perhaps the inner world will stay quiet.

But talk reveals even when it tries to hide.

The more unchecked the speech the clearer the wound beneath it becomes. Control disguised as advice. Superiority dressed up as storytelling. Validation-seeking masquerading as information. In many cases the person speaking has no relationship with silence at all. They do not know how to sit without commentary. They do not trust presence to carry them. So they fill every space with explanation.

And in doing so they take something from others. Not intentionally perhaps but consistently.

Listening under these conditions becomes emotional labor. You regulate the room by staying calm.
You hold your reactions.
You minimise your needs.
You postpone your own expression.
Over time this does something subtle.. but damaging.
It teaches you that your voice requires permission. That your thoughts are interruptions. That your inner life must wait until someone else is finished with theirs.

This dynamic becomes especially powerful when the chronically loquacious person holds authority.

A parent.. A family elder.. A provider..A Person senior in hierarchy..
Someone whose voice is culturally protected and rarely questioned.

In such spaces words are no longer just excessive. They are imprisoning.

There are places where speech does not invite dialogue but enforces hierarchy. Where one voice fills the room like smoke and everyone else breathes it quietly.
The commentary never stops.
On food.. On finances.. On choices..
On perceived failures.. On imagined obligations..
Even moments meant for rest are hijacked by analysis and instruction.

In these work places and homes silence is not peace. Silence is strategy.
It is how you survive until you can leave.
Children in these environments do not learn how to speak clearly.
They learn how to disappear.
Spouses learn how to nod without agreeing.
Everyone learns how to live with a running commentary that never considers whether it is welcome.

The damage here is not loud. It is slow. It is the erosion of self trust. The shrinking of internal space. The belief that having a thought does not automatically grant you the right to express it.

This is not just about irritation. It is about oxygen.

People who live under chronic verbal domination are not craving freedom in abstract terms. They are craving the right to breathe without being explained to. To exist without being narrated. To have a moment where no one is shaping their reality through constant speech.

And eventually something shifts..

Sometimes the departure is physical.
Sometimes it is emotional.

One day the listener stops engaging.
Not dramatically.. Not loudly.. Just quietly..

They withdraw their energy. Their curiosity. Their availability. And the talker is often shocked. They do not understand why the room feels empty. Why people leave earlier. Why conversations end sooner. Why calls go unanswered.

They mistake endurance for connection and silence for agreement.

Not all chronically loquacious people are the same. The intention varies but the impact often overlaps.

Some speak to dominate. They interrupt. They override. They believe the loudest voice carries truth. Others just perform.
They need reaction.. ..Laughter ..Admiration Attention.. as proof of worth.
Some ramble from insecurity. They speak in circles afraid that stopping will expose their inadequacy.
Others preach. They advise without invitation. They assume authority over lives they do not fully understand.
Some overshare from unhealed pain spilling stories that demand emotional holding from unwilling listeners.
Others criticise compulsively, filling space with judgment because it keeps them from feeling powerless.

And some simply cannot tolerate silence at all. They narrate weather.. Traffic.. Nothing....Anything Just to avoid stillness.

Different wounds..Same exhaustion on the other side.

If you are reading this and recognise yourself as someone who often speaks too much, this is not condemnation.
It is an invitation to notice.
Notice what rises when you pause.
Notice the discomfort that arrives when you do not fill space immediately.

Ask yourself what you are protecting. What you fear might surface if you let silence stay.

Presence does not require performance. Worth does not depend on word count. Wisdom is not measured by how long you can hold the floor.

Learning to pause is not about diminishing yourself. It is about expanding the room so others can exist fully inside it too.

And if you are someone who has lived as the listener, the absorber, the one who always holds space while their own voice waits, there is something here for you as well.

Silence can be sacred. But silence without choice becomes suppression.. and suppression always turns into resentment.

You are allowed to interrupt.
You are allowed to redirect.
You are allowed to say you need space.
You are allowed to stop listening.
Boundaries are not cruelty. They are clarity and clarity is what keeps relationships honest.

Types of Chronically Loquacious People

~ And the invisible energies they leak into every room

1. The Dominator

"If I speak louder, I win."
Uses talking as a tool of control and authority
Interrupts, dismisses others' views, often uses aggressive tone masked as "truth" or "advice"
Subconscious Need to feel Powerful. This person believes if they stop speaking, they lose control.

Impact on others: Intimidation, shrinking of self-esteem, internalised fear of speaking.
Typical Avatar: Controlling parents, rigid elders, corporate bullies, insecure spouses

2. The Performer

"Let me entertain you… endlessly."
Talks to stay liked, admired, and validated
Loud, dramatic, over-detailed, constant storytelling, even where it's irrelevant
Subconscious Need for Approval and applause
Impact on Others: Emotional fatigue, loss of attention, inability to relax in their presence
Typical Avatar: Friends who dominate group dynamics, attention-seeking partners

3. The Insecure Rambler

"If I stop, I'll be judged."
Talks nervously and compulsively, overshares everything
Disorganised, repetitive, filled with disclaimers, self-deprecating jokes
Subconscious Need for Acceptance and not feeling left out or stupid
Impact on Others: Compassion fatigue, second-hand anxiety, mental clutter
Typical Avatar: People pleasers, social outsiders trying to belong

4. The Self-Appointed Guru

"Let me enlighten you whether you asked or not."
Speaks in monologues, thinks they know it all
Preachy, over-advising, condescending tone, unsolicited "wisdom".

Subconscious Need for Superiority and being the 'go-to' person.
Impact on Others: Guilt, confusion, suppression of individual voice
Typical Avatar: Overbearing teachers, elders who refuse to update, wellness "experts" with no listening ear

5. The Wounded Oversharer

"If I spill it all, you'll finally see my pain."
Talks emotionally, sometimes without boundaries, trauma-dumps
Raw, personal, sometimes inappropriate or overly intense
Subconscious Need to be seen, to feel their suffering matters
Impact on Others: Emotional overwhelm, silent resentment, blurred boundaries
Typical Avatar: Friends in prolonged victim loops, unhealed individuals seeking space but taking energy

6. The Chronic Critic

"Let me tell you what's wrong with everything and everyone."
Talks to complain, judge, or compare
Cynical, sarcastic, rarely constructive
Subconscious Need.. Feels powerless and projects that frustration outward
Impact on Others: Lowers vibration, spreads negativity, emotional depletion
Typical Avatar: Family members who gossip endlessly, elders stuck in old paradigms

7. The Conversational Hoarder

"Every second of silence is a threat."
Fills every pause with talk, cannot tolerate silence
Pointless details, weather updates, unnecessary commentary

Subconscious Need for Avoidance of inner dialogue, fear of feeling
Impact on Others: Claustrophobia, blocked intuition, frustration in deep thinkers
Typical Avatar: Neighbours, relatives, coworkers who talk just to talk

Here's a Closing Thought..

Every talker tells a story… not of what they say but of why they must keep saying it.
And every listener holds a mirror…reflecting the emotional cost of unchecked noise.

My Showdown

In many closed doors, speech is not shared. It is imposed.
Advice is given without invitation. Commentary replaces curiosity. Silence becomes the safest response, not because there is peace but because resistance feels costly.

In such spaces, people don't lose their voice all at once. They lose it gradually.
Sentence by sentence. Thought by thought.

No one calls it abuse. No one calls it control.
But everyone feels the weight of it.
This was my showdown. Realising that words can suffocate just as deeply as silence can.

And I've been on both sides of this dynamic..
There were times I spoke too much because I needed to feel relevant. Because I was afraid my presence alone was not enough.
And there were times I stayed silent while someone else filled every room because it felt easier than confronting the imbalance.

Both left me empty.

What changed was not technique. It was awareness.
I began to notice how words feel in the body. How some conversations leave you nourished and others leave you tense.
How true connection has ..Rhythm ..Exchange ..Breath

The most important thing I learned was that exhaustion after conversation is information..!

It is not moodiness.. It is not oversensitivity.. It is feedback..

The body knows when it has not been met.

I learned that listening without boundaries slowly turns into resentment. And resentment corrodes relationships silently.

I learned that silence is sacred only when it is chosen. When it is enforced, it becomes suppression.

I also learned to look honestly at myself. At the moments when I over-explained. When I spoke to fill insecurity. When I used words to prove instead of to connect.

I realised that not every thought needs expression.
And not every silence needs filling.

G^3 Goonj~

The most powerful conversations I have experienced were not loud.
They were spacious.. They allowed pauses..
They allowed difference.. They allowed mutual existence.

This is the invitation of this chapter..
Here is what I hold now and what I offer you gently.

If you speak a lot, practice pausing. Not as a technique but as a form of respect.
Let silence sit long enough for someone else to arrive.

You may discover that your presence is felt even when your words stop.

If you listen a lot, practice speaking early.
Not when frustration has already built.
Your voice deserves space before it has to fight for it.

Notice how conversations make you feel after they end. That feeling is your compass.

Connection is not measured by how much is said.
It is measured by how much room is created.

Words are powerful but space is what makes them meaningful.

And sometimes the most healing thing you can do for yourself is recognise this simple truth.

You are not here to disappear so someone else can stay comfortable.
But..
To speak with intention rather than compulsion.
To listen with presence rather than endurance.
To recognise that words are tools not weapons and silence is not absence but possibility.

Not everyone who talks is wise.
Not everyone who is quiet is lost.

But those who learn when to speak and when to pause carry something rare..
A presence that does not suffocate.
A voice that does not dominate.
A silence that feels like permission.

That is the language worth mastering..!

CHAPTER 15

SHOWDOWN WITH ROASTING YOURSELF

~EVERY TIME YOU GOSSIP YOU'RE ACTUALLY ROASTING YOURSELF

Gossip feels good for a moment. That brief release is what hooks people. It gives a sense of connection relief even power. And all this comes at a cost most people never notice. When you gossip you are not processing someone else. You are training your own mind body and energy to turn against you.
Every word you release lands back on your nervous system. Every judgment reshapes how you are perceived and how you perceive yourself.
Gossip is not commentary. It is self-exposure.
And most people are unaware they are the ones being revealed.

Here's the Brain's Dirty Trick..
There is a neurological phenomenon with a fancy name.

Spontaneous Trait Transfer.

In plain language it means…
Whatever label you assign out loud your brain quietly accepts as self-description.

You say she's fake. Your brain records fake and tags it inward.
You whisper he's insecure. Your nervous system hears insecure and files it under identity.

What makes it worse is this. The people listening do the same thing.
They do not remember the person you described. They remember you as the one who speaks that way.

You walk away thinking you were clever…
No..you leave behind a residue of…

Jealous..Petty..Bitter..Untrustworthy.

No announcement. No warning. Just a quiet recalibration of how you are perceived.

I lived this..

Bangalore taught me a strange language. Smiles in the front. Knives at the back.

People promised the moon at dinner and forgot your name by breakfast. Not out of cruelty.. out of convenience.

I found myself at gatherings where absence became currency. Someone stepped out and suddenly they were the menu.

At first I only listened. Uncomfortable.. ..Uneasy
Wondering why I was even there.

It was never dramatic gossip. Nothing scandalous. Just the casual dissection.
Did you notice how she dresses.
Did you feel his energy was off.

Then one evening mid-laughter something snapped.
I realised I wasn't talking about her. I was talking about me.

Every comment I made was a confession in disguise.
Every judgment a fear I hadn't owned.

The more I mocked inconsistency the more I revealed my terror of being seen as unreliable.

The more I sneered at fakery the more I feared my own masks slipping.
The gossip was not social. It was psychological.
It was a mirror I kept turning away from.

Sacred Spaces that aren't so sacred..
What shook me most was not the parties.
It was the spiritual circles.

You expect gossip in living rooms and lounges. You don't expect it wrapped in concern and offered as guidance.

I sat among seekers who leaned in and whispered..
"I'm only saying this because I care" and then they
proceeded to undress someone who wasn't even there,
to speak for themselves.
It wasn't feedback. It was surgical gossip dressed in saffron.

That disturbed me deeply.

Educated women.. Financially independent.. Spiritually literate.
Still poisoning the room with absence-based judgment.
Picky..Cruel..Sabotaging

I remember thinking if this is how we treat unseen souls in sacred spaces what frequency are we actually building.
I had come looking for refuge from my own battles.
I thought I was safe there.

I wasn't..
Because gossip doesn't care where you sit. It only cares that you speak.

Now..the Moment Awareness Arrived..
The more I understood energy the clearer it became. Gossip was not about them. It was a toxin dripping into me.

A self-inflicted branding exercise.
Every word a stamp. Every sentence a poster. Advertising a version of me I didn't want to be.

This was not morality.. This was mechanics.

You say she's desperate. Your system hears desperate and adjusts accordingly.
You say he lacks integrity. Your field absorbs the frequency of integrity loss.
Zero cost.. Maximum damage..

My Showdown

There was a night when it all stopped.

Another gathering.. Another circle.. Another round of names tossed like darts.
This time I went silent.

I watched faces animate with judgment. I listened to laughter sharpen into cruelty.

Then the real thought arrived. Cold. Precise.
If I weren't here tonight I would be the next name.

Absence is an open invitation. Gossip doesn't need villains. It needs empty chairs.

That was the knife twist.
And yet something else rose with it.

Even when people hurt me cornered me betrayed me tested my patience until it broke, I had still resisted gossip.

Did I slip sometimes. Yes.. Especially when pain needed processing and truth needed air.

But even then I tried to understand not wound.

That's when it became undeniable.
Gossip was never my language.
I didn't stop gossiping to be "better."
I stopped because I saw that every sentence was training my brain, body and field in a direction I didn't consent to.

The real showdown wasn't me versus gossipers. It was me versus the temptation to belong where I didn't belong.

So I chose differently.
I chose discomfort over contamination..
I chose silence…I chose exit.

When someone baited me with
Don't you think she's…

I answered..
I don't talk about people when they're not here.

A sudden shift in the room…

People grew uneasy.. Some called me too serious..
Eventually the invitations thinned. And I was delicately shifted out of their mailing list..

And that was the price.
Exile over poison.. Frequency over familiarity..

One thing of utmost focus..

Body Remembers What the Mouth Repeats..

Here is what I had missed earlier and what matters deeply.
Gossip does not stay in the mind. It settles in the body.

Every unspoken fear carried through words tightens the chest.
Every repeated judgment hardens the jaw.
Every whispered insult contracts the gut.

The body does not understand sarcasm or social games.
It only understands vibration.

What you repeat becomes posture.
What you speak becomes tension.
What you judge becomes weight.
I was amazed to see how karma theory works..
This is why gossip exhausts people.
As they carry the energetic cost of their own speech.

Words are as equal to Spells..

Science explains the wiring. Spirit explains the consequence.

Words are not neutral. They are instructions.
Every insult becomes an affirmation. Every judgment a rope around your own subconscious.
You are not describing reality. You are programming it.

Gossip corrupts your social image and your spiritual frequency simultaneously.

That is its genius and its cruelty.

There is another layer we rarely talk about.

The Ancestral Layer..

Gossip is often inherited.
Many of us grew up in homes where absence was discussed freely and presence was avoided. Where silence around pain turned into commentary about others.

When you stop gossiping you are not just changing behaviour. You are interrupting lineage.

When you are say this pattern ends with me.
That matters more than you realise.

The Gunj Gyaan..

Let me be blunt.

Gossip is cowardice disguised as wit. It is shadow boxing with your own insecurity while pretending you're superior.

I would rather sit alone with clean energy than dine at a table where reputations are the main course.

The next time you feel the urge pause.

Ask yourself..
Is this about them or is this about something in me asking to be seen..?

Because the real showdown is never with her or him. It is with the version of you that keeps setting yourself on fire and calling it conversation.

I didn't stop gossiping to be kinder. I stopped because I realised something far more confronting.

Every time I spoke about someone who wasn't present I was rehearsing a version of myself I didn't respect. I was lending my voice to rooms that fed on absence and calling it connection. I was mistaking familiarity for belonging and the longer I stayed the more counterfeit I felt.

So I chose differently.
I chose silence over spice.. Distance over participation.. Integrity over inclusion..

Some circles dissolved. Others quietly disappeared. Nothing dramatic happened.
No confrontations.. No explanations..

Just a recalibration of.. where my energy was willing to sit.
And that was enough.

I stopped gossiping not to be kind but because I refused to keep advertising a version of myself I did not respect.

CHAPTER 16

SHOWDOWN WITH ABANDONMENT

~BETRAYAL IN THE ROOM WHERE LIFE BEGINS

It is not merely a story of childbirth.
It is the story of abandonment at the most fragile threshold of existence,
when one hovers between life and death, between silence and screams, between blackout and awakening.
The emotions that surfaced were not gentle, but raw and primal, rising straight from the core of survival itself.

I still remember the puffiness of my body the folds around my neck, the water retention in my legs, the patches across my skin. Nine months of fighting to keep a fragile pregnancy alive with painful injections, with weight piling on, with a body that didn't feel mine anymore. Yet none of that prepared me for what was to come the hour when I would be left abandoned, bleeding, and unheard in a room that was supposed to be a sanctuary for new life.

The due date passed. Then another day. And another.
Every trip to the doctor meant more waiting, more uncertainty, more exhaustion. When labor finally came, it was not graceful it was brutal, six hours of wrestling with pain so sharp it split through the marrow of my bones.
'Epidural'… NO WAY… went all in..
All natural..

After struggling for more than six hours the final push was not born of strength, not the Doctors words that scared but of desperation the sound of my baby's heart rate falling was the only thing that forced me past the limit of human endurance.

And then…blackness.

I was there, but not there. Wide awake inside, but blind to the world outside. Whether it was the shock of the final push, the collapse from massive blood loss, or my body shutting down to survive, my sight simply vanished and darkness took over blurring my world completely.
I could hear the congratulations, I could feel my husband's kiss but I couldn't see my child.
All I saw was a void. My body gave birth but my soul was still teetering between worlds.

The doctor left for an "emergency."
The nurses disappeared. And I was left, legs high on leg holder , blood dripping, body torn open, alone in that labor room.
Time slowed..
The clock on the wall became my only companion, ticking so loud, the minutes of my abandonment.
When I opened my eyes again, it was more than an hour later. Blood had pooled beneath me. Clots the size of fists were spilling out. My voice screamed for help, but the walls swallowed it.

Somehow, I released legs from those holders myself.. pulled my trembling body upright.
Somehow, I turned a plastic chair into my walker and began the longest walk of my life.. a walk of blood..every step..
Every step I took, another clot bomb, hit the floor with a heavy splash, a sound that still haunts me. I left a trail of red, proof that I existed, that I was fighting not to collapse.

The nurses looked at me with shock, as if I had walked out of the grave.
"Are you okay?" they asked, while my blood was flooding the corridor. This wasn't care. This was betrayal.

When the doctor finally returned hours later, her mask was still streaked with someone else's blood. She looked at me and said I was "creating drama." Drama. I was standing there, drained of life, begging to be seen and that was her word.

upon examining me she realised the blunder and I was rushed to OT eventually.
I heard the announcements calling my family. I was parked on a stretcher and saw the panicked steps of my mother.. signing forms because my husband wasn't there. I hugged my two-year-old daughter, not knowing if I would return.
My simple mom-in-law all lost wondering what's happening at this time of celebration.. a boy right !!

And in those moments before anaesthesia, I thought this might be the end…

As I went under anaesthesia, I actually drifted between realms again.
My body numbed, but my consciousness awake.
I heard their conversations as they stitched me up, cauterised the tear, sealed the bleeding.
Somewhere between their clinical orders and hurried hands to seal the haemorrhage, I realised how close I had come to vanishing.

That night, as blood transfusions kept me tethered to this earth, I lay awake not only in the restless weakness but in grief.
Not for the pain of childbirth but for the pain of abandonment.
For being treated as if I didn't matter, as if my screams were fiction, as if my body was disposable.

That walk did not end in that corridor. It quietly rewired my relationship with safety and authority for years to come.

After that day, my body learned not to wait, not to assume rescue, not to surrender its knowing to uniforms or titles. As I dragged myself through blood, I met the part of me that would never wait to be rescued again.
I was not being saved. I was saving myself.. I name this not to accuse but to record...because that moment became a blueprint forever etched into my subconscious.

And when my son was finally placed beside me, he did not cry.
He was breathing. A slow, steady breath against my skin, his fingers curling once around mine, anchoring me back into the living world.
Life returned in the gentlest way and I finally saw his face. His tiny breaths, his fragile warmth, his sacred presence pressed against me. His cheek to my cheek..
Tears rolled, unstoppable.
I had walked through darkness, through blood, through betrayal but I had walked back into love.

This experience hollowed me.
It tore deeper than the scalpel, deeper than the stitches, deeper than the blood loss.
That was the wound that truly took my breath away.

G^3 Goonj~

Because what happened to me was not fate, it was not destiny. It was negligence...plain and undeniable.
So even after so many years the pain is still fresh
In year 2000, was under the care of **Dr. Shetty,** at a famous hospital in Bangalore, a hospital that prides on its reputation as a premier "metro-city" institution.

Yet, in my most fragile hour, I was left alone. After the birth of my son, the lady doctor stepped away for another case and the nurses followed. For more than two hours, I remained there bleeding, my legs still strapped in labor position, untreated, unattended, unseen.

When help finally arrived, it came not with comfort, but with dismissal. My collapse, the blood loss, the fading in and out of consciousness was reduced to a single word "Drama."
A word that still echoes, sharper than any scalpel. If I had not forced my body upright, dragging myself through the corridor, blood marking every step, I may not have survived to tell this story.

And then came another quiet wound. Without a word to me, the hospital assigned my newborn to **Dr. Shetty** the forced paediatrician and husband of the very doctor who had walked away.
A seamless handover within their circle of authority, framed as care but steeped in assumption.
I was not consulted.. I was not heard..
In those moments, I was not a mother..they had turned me into a case file and my son into a transaction.

Abandonment is not just about being left in that room. It is the wound of being unseen when you need to be seen the most. It is the betrayal of trust when care is promised but denied. That day, I was not only torn in flesh, I was torn in spirit.

Because beyond the pain of childbirth and the terror of blood loss, there was a deeper agony…the void of not seeing my newborn's face..That emptiness.. cut deeper than any wound.
The thought that I might have slipped away without even one glimpse of my child was unbearable. It hollowed me from the inside.

But even in that hollow, alone, almost erased… I met the darkness and the Darkness made me discover something so valuable..

When the world forgets you, even when the system betrays you, even when your voice goes unheard… your soul will still fight for life. Your body will walk through blood. Your spirit will crawl through voids and your heart will return, just in time, to kiss the face of love.

I kept on searched for meaning in karma and destiny but meaning does not erase responsibility. What unfolded was not divine play but human neglect at a moment that demanded care.

That day, I not only survived the neglect. But more than survival, I claimed a deeper truth… Divinity does not ever abandon. Ever !

That moment stitched me back into life. That embrace taught me that Divinity never abandons.. it waits,
sometimes through unbearable voids, to return us to love.

So.. when I finally kissed my son's tiny fist, tears came streaming down my face..
I understood…
I had not only brought him into this world.. I had brought myself back to life. And the moment I held him close to my chest, I knew I had crossed the threshold of death for this precious life that I hold in my arms, for this precious moment that will write an extraordinary story of his life as he's not an ordinary and I only a medium !

CHAPTER 17

SHOWDOWN WITH THE RAW SCAR

~TARGETED BY AUTHORITY

I was five.. in Upper KG, a fragile little girl with long pigtails, oversized socks and a pencil that felt heavier than my whole body.

And then there was **Mrs. McIntosh**.
Her anger entered the classroom before her feet did. You could feel it.. that disciplined, suffocating air, that hush that settled like a funeral silence the moment she touched the doorknob.
We were kids but even children know when to hold their breath.

For some reason, she had her eyes on me.
Maybe because my hand couldn't keep up with the speed of her chalk.
Maybe because my *d's* looked like *b's* in cursive, my *b's* like *d's*.
Dyslexia, perhaps, but in those days nobody knew such words.
Nobody cared.
All everyone cared was punish her..do laga do..

She came to me everyday and in some sense I was her target..
one day, she picked up my notebook and hissed, in her very British accent,

"What have you written, Kunshan?"
That accent reeked discrimination to what extend I can't describe..!

Before I could gather my breath or understand my pounding heart or utter, she snatched my pencil, sharpened it and then poked it into my skull.
Yes. Into my head.. Not a metaphor.. Not a child's exaggeration.. Real.. The graphite tip breaking skin, the lesson carved not into paper but into me.
And exactly…same spot, which I will unravel later..

That was English, as she taught it.
Not language.. Not poetry.. But fear..an early grammar etched with pain.

By the time I reached Class 6th, I met the deadliest scar.. **Mrs. Fernandez**, the mathematics teacher.
With her, numbers weren't numbers. They were failures, waiting with sharpened teeth.
She didn't just fail me in math tests.. She failed me in identity..

Her voice still echoes:
"Gandi ladki." You Dirty girl.

If I was caught whispering to a friend?
"**Gandi ladki, class ke bahar khadi ho ja.** Dirty girl, go stand outside the class."

There were others too involved in that whisper but I was the one targeted.

Imagine being a eleven-year-old girl, already confused by your own body changing, now baptised with a name that stains.
Dirty girl.. Dirty girl.. Dirty girl..
It used to constantly ring in my ears even the days I didn't have maths.
I began to believe it.. Not just in school.. ..Everywhere

Later in life..came **Mrs. D'Souza**, our drawing teacher.

A woman always wrapped in starched saris, thick glasses and a cough that preceded her like an announcement. Cough, cough, cough and the whole class would whisper, she's here..!

I loved colours. Water colours were my refuge, my tiny rebellion against all the greyness around me. I shaded with life, with soul, with something bigger than a child's hands should have known.
But she never saw it. Never approved.
Her eyes only found brightness in papers less alive, strokes less steady, work less felt. I poured myself onto every page and every page came back to me rejected.

Art, which could have been my sanctuary, became another battlefield where my worth was dismissed.
But in finals..another teacher was grading..and I got 85/100..
I was too innocent to even understand the difference but only happy that I was getting better..

But before all of this… came my brother.
I was as young as three. Too young to even spell the word **pain**, yet old enough to feel it crawl inside my skin.
He tortured me in the dark hours of night.
And when the torment ended, he would wipe my tears, tuck me into bed, kiss my forehead, and whisper..
"When mama and papa come, don't tell them. You're a nice girl. You're my nice sister. My baby sister.
Don't share this with mummy and papa, because bhaiya loves you my little sister."

And I believed him. Because I wanted to be loved. Because I wanted to be "nice."
That's the first survival skill I learned.. **to hide.**
To hide my tears..To hide my fears.. To swallow my screams before they left my throat.

At three years old, I had already mastered the art of **shape-shifting…**coming out in the morning with a smile, while my pillow still smelled of last night's sobs.

And this is how my life began shaping.
Every word they hurled in school became another chain around my tongue. Every insult, every dismissal, every stab it all found a place in the wound my brother had carved first.
I learned to expect cruelty, even when it wasn't coming.

So, I grew up wearing the mask of an extrovert, but inside I had already folded into silence.
I learned to take shit quietly, because somewhere deep inside I knew that if I spoke, someone would spit words like knives.
Even if it didn't happen, I expected it.. I lived over-cautious, over-careful.

That little girl turned into a woman who walked on eggshells through her own life.
In early marriage,
I didn't fight.. I didn't argue.. I accepted.. I absorbed.. I bent..
Because my childhood had taught me that resistance only brings punishment. That speaking only sharpens pencils into weapons.

Psychology calls it trauma..
I call it a **RAW SCAR'S ..!**
A scar that never erased, that never faded and still breathing with me through every decade.

And now, in my late forties, I look back.
I see how those teachers…those self-appointed gods of the classroom, carved their fear into me. How my brother rehearsed me into silence before I could even read.
How all of them together stitched their anger, their cruelty, their secrets into my personality.

But here's the **Showdown:**
I am still here.
The scar is raw, but it's also proof I survived.
Proof that I endured. Proof that even when they tried to break me into silence,
I carried on breathing, writing, painting, living..

This scar doesn't define me anymore..
And today, I write it not as the child they tried to wound
but as the woman who refused to stay their "dirty girl."

G³ Goonj~
If you've carried scars from childhood, let me tell you something they never did..
You are not dirty.. You are not weak.. You are not broken..
You are the soul who learned to smile while bleeding, who learned to shape-shift in order to survive. That survival skill is not shame.. it is genius..!

But survival isn't living.
At some point, you must look at the scar.. raw, trembling, alive.
Instead of hiding it, you must name it. Touch it.. Write it.. Own it..

Because scars are not proof of your weakness.
They are proof of your survival.
And when you finally face them, they stop being chains and start being your liberation.

"The scar they gave me is my **Kintsugi** , a golden crack that turned my wound into light and that light is my calling and your healing**." G³**

I've a feeling this quote just crowns it !
And so, every scar that burned me, every silence that choked me, every word that cut me…they did not end me.
They shaped me.

They were not tombstones..They were chisels.

Because all the pain I endured and all the resilience I gathered, became the hidden current that now fuels me.
They became the quiet, insistent **nudge of the universe** that pushed me into my calling… into being a natural born guide.

I did not study healing in a classroom.
I lived it..I bled it..I carried it in my bones.

I know the tremor in your voice when you say, "I'm fine," but you're breaking inside.
I know the silence behind your tears, when you cry in secret because the world won't understand.
I know that scream trapped behind your sigh, because I've been there and I walked through it barefoot, alone, in the dark.

That is why I can see you in a crowd..
You, who are carrying invisible wounds.
You, who are suffering quietly, waiting for someone to notice.
You, who need salvation, not in the grand sense of temples or scriptures but in the tender sense of finally being seen.

I know you.
Because I was you.

And today, I heal not because I read about pain, but because I was forged in it.
I heal not because I chose it as a career, because life carved it into me as a destiny.

This is the showdown with the RAW SCAR.
And here I stand…not as a victim of it, but as the alchemist of it.
Not only alive but awake.
Not only awake but here to awaken..

And if you are reading this with a scar throbbing inside you then know this:

your scar too can speak..
your scar too can heal..
your scar too can become the very proof that you were always meant to rise..

CHAPTER 18

SHOWDOWN WITH HELPLESSNESS

~A WIFE, A MOTHER, A HEALER INSIDE THE APOCALYPSE

There was a time when helplessness wasn't an occasional visitor in my life.

Not the obvious kind you see in movies, not the screaming, running kind but the slow, choking kind. The helplessness of being unseen, unheard, unprepared. The helplessness of watching your world burn and not knowing if water even exists.

I thought fear was my biggest enemy. But when COVID hit, I realised it wasn't fear. It was helplessness.

Fear screams.. helplessness stays silent. .And silence can kill.

It sat in my chest like a weight and refused to leave.

I used to think fear was my worst enemy. I was wrong. Fear shouts. Helplessness whispers. And the whisper becomes a chokehold.

COVID didn't just arrive at our door as a virus. It came as a black tide, carrying denial, exhaustion, shortages, silence. It came as an apocalypse disguised as a pandemic.

It started quietly, the way all storms do.

My husband, Nirmal burning down with with fever.

Refusing tests.. Refusing rest.. Refusing to believe..

Refusing to admit that something larger than him was moving through his body. I watched him sweat, cough, shiver and yet say, "I'm fine."

Denial is its own disease. And I was guilty of it too. Hoping it was just exhaustion. Hoping it would pass.I wanted to believe him. I wanted to believe my own denial. But the oximeter numbers started sliding and my chest constricted with every digit that dropped.

Fear was everywhere in our minds, in the news, even in the silence of hospitals turning us away.

His spo2 was dropping, and I had to do what no heart wants to do

Put my foot down. Make a call !

Myself, my son, my daughter & her friend after much debate we took a decision to shift him to a hospital immediately.. it was challenging to convince my husband at first but finally he accepted

And just before midnight,

The ambulance came just before midnight. They wouldn't take me. I wasn't allowed inside as I had no symptoms and there was no exception.

So I stood on the street with my daughter and son clutching, watching him enter the van…with faint hope and a fragile thread of faith we let him go in that van driven not by a medic but by fate...

My family split in two by a virus that thrived in silence. I felt like my heart was being driven away with him. Into a night where nothing was certain and everything was waiting.

As he arrived at the hospital only to know about the broken lift.!

A midnight climb.

Five strangers dragging his weak body on a stretcher up dark staircases. I wasn't there to hold his hand. I heard it later. I saw every stumble, I was on video call with him..

Inside the hospital there was uncertainty dressed as protocol. Courteous staff but no readiness as no one knew how to begin the treatment as the drugs on the virus was not experimented before

However.. First aid was administered with my consent but no plan. Heart racing…panic rising… I was shocked how I send him to an ordinary hospital

So with lot of calls entire night for a better reputed hospital transfer.

Only to find refusals.. Rude voices.. Cold hands..Unreasonable demands..

"No beds. No doctors. No rooms."

This was not the news. This was not television. This was my husband. My family.

I called friends. My brother Pulled strings. Reached MDs. Begged. Finally, a room. And a fragile breath of relief. But relief evaporated quickly in that atmosphere.

Wait.. the Apocalypse was yet to arrive..

By day I was a warrior !

Hospitals, bills, forms, oxygen cylinders, blood banks stacked with desperate people. Pharmacies shut with zero stocks. Streets echoing with the sounds of crying, yelling, loss. Doctors themselves with brain fog, guessing treatments, trying to hold humanity together.

By evening I was back to run the kitchen. Feeding my children, feeding helpers, making sure nobody starved while our world cracked.

By night, while others slept..

I was on the phone… making calls to doctors in the city, outside the city, outside the country.

Calling: my niece, Dr Manjit Tahiliani & Dr Harsh Tahiliani, her husband are well renowned doctors in mumbai, begging for guidance at 1am , 3 am, 4 am…

My Children's paediatrician Dr Sandip another god send angel took my calls in. Every inconvenient time I called..

Dr Ajay Chaugle, Cardiologist, a gem of a human being.

Dr Satish Amarnath, Microbiologist, truly Godsend, arranged the room in the hospital..

These doctors, who were themselves exhausted, found time for me in their off hours. That was God's grace disguised as humanity.. people from inside my nexus and outside, both guiding me, keeping me two steps ahead.

My own sixth sense combined with their wisdom. Together, it became my weapon. Because at that time, anyone with 80% lung damage did not make it out alive. That was the reality. That was the apocalypse we were living. I refused to let Nirmal become another statistic.

Then came the horrific Collapse

At 4 am the hospital called.

His lungs had collapsed. They needed my consent for immediate ventilation.

I stood frozen in the dark, phone in one hand, life in the other.

Sleep had already left my body. For three months I did not know what it meant to sleep. My eyes stayed open long after the sun rose. My pulse raced long after the calls ended.

What if saying YES killed him..? What if saying NO killed him..?

That's what helplessness is…being forced to choose between deaths.

Shiva I surrender …Yes !

Five days on ventilation..Five days of despair followed..

Back-to-back Video calls with nurses at odd hours..

Hearing his voice break.. Seeing his body wired.. Nurses yelling & torturing as he was resisting treatment… somewhere he stilled believed he was fine and it was not covid.

Me whispering through a screen, "You're not alone. Hold on Jaan. Please hold on."

Then came Faith and Fury Together..

We were all positive.. My children.. ..Myself My helpers..

But no symptoms.

Just racing hearts. Just sleepless nights. Protected by something bigger than us.

I carried the virus, but also carried medicines across cities, papers across hospitals, prayers across dimensions.

Hanuman Chalisa seven times daily. Repetitive Chaupai Sahib paths. 108 Maha Mrityunjay jaaps, all in continuous loop..

Any ritual anyone suggested, I followed.

For me logic had collapsed only faith remained.

At night, in between calls, I cried quietly. And then picked up the phone again.

Then cried some more. It was a rhythm fear, prayer, action, tears.

For three months, he fought in ICU.

For three months, I fought outside.

Financial collapse loomed. I swallowed my pride, sold jewellery, asked for help.

In those times, a few deeply kind, friends and family extended their support and generosity in their own ways.

Me, who never asked anything from anyone.

Me, who always gave..

This was another death.. death of My Ego.

That was the biggest death of all…My pride.

I saw patients left alone. I saw families crying in parking lots. I saw rude nurses, helpless doctors, protocols without kindness.

And I realised everyone was suffering. Everyone was helpless.

My pain wasn't mine alone it was the pain of a world cracking open.

And yet, in that breaking, something else surged multifold.. ..Compassion ..Empathy ..Fire

Three months later, Nirmal came home. Twenty kilos lighter. Fragile.

Lungs scarred. But alive.

He says he was a guinea pig.

I say he was a warrior.

And I..? I was not the same woman who watched that ambulance drive away. I came back scarred but softened. Stronger, but more porous. I came back seeing suffering not as something to avoid, but as something to hold.

G³ Goonj~

Helplessness was my teacher.

Fear didn't break me. Fear taught me presence. But helplessness cracked me open into compassion.

People watched COVID on television screens. I lived it in my living room, my kitchen, innumerable phone calls in my room and my tears.

And in that furnace, the empath in me was further put through grit.

Now, when I heal, I don't heal from theory. I heal from lived fire. I heal because I know what it is to stand alone in the dark, to pray without words, to hope against science, to beg God with mantras, to be refused, to be unseen and still rise.

Helplessness taught me that healing isn't about becoming fearless.

It's about not abandoning yourself.

Not abandoning your people.. Not abandoning love.

If ever…you are in the middle of the dark, trembling and waiting..

Remember!

You are not broken…You are not lost..

Believe…You are fire.. And fire rises..!

CHAPTER 19

SHOWDOWN WITH GUILT

~A CRY FROM THE SOUL OF EVERY CHILD

A letter to parents..

Parents…
Do you know what guilt sounds like?

It's not always born inside us.
Sometimes… it is stitched into us, thread by thread,
by the very people who raised us.

Not from cruelty.. but from concern.
Not from hatred.. but from fear.
And yet… the wound is the same.

Many parents begin parenting long before a child arrives.
They parent from guilt.
Guilt of scarcity..
Guilt of absence.. masked as responsibility.
Guilt of the life… they postponed so their children could move forward.
That guilt does not dissolve on its own.
It seeps into tone..Into expectation..Into comparison dressed up as care.
And without knowing it parents try to quiet their own regret by demanding flawlessness from the lives that carry their name.

"You have everything. Why aren't you doing better?"
"Look at others. Look how far they've reached."
"We've given you everything. And still… this?"

You think you're motivating us.
We only hear condemning us.
You think it's care.We only feel shame.
Your voice becomes our inner critic.
Your sigh becomes our anxiety.
Your concern becomes our cage.

Yes… you carried burdens.. Yes… you sacrificed.
But hear this..

We are not your second chance at life.
We are not your redemption song.
We are not born to pay you back with perfection.

We are here…
to stumble..to rise..to breathe..to be.
But what you don't see is this..

We cry ourselves to sleep.
We avoid your eyes after failure.
We hide our dreams because we know your tone will crush them before they take shape.

Looking for refuge, not always realising they're running from an invisible war inside.
Because once the fight-or-flight instinct is activated in a child not once.. but repeatedly it doesn't just vanish.
It becomes a mental trigger.
A ticking loop..

Any confrontation, any rejection, any moment that smells like guilt or shame..
Their system screams… RUN !

They RUN from friendships.
They RUN from commitment.
They RUN from guidance.
They RUN from anything that looks remotely like a judgment zone.

Not because they're flaky.
Not because they're spoiled.
But because their nervous system was trained to survive, not to thrive.

Not because we want to ruin our lives.
But because guilt blurred our vision of truth.

Dear parents…
Most children don't fight you..They leave you.

Not because they don't love you.
But because the version of you that comes with judgment
hurts more than it hugs.

Your dining table..? It feels like a courtroom.
Your home..? A prison.
Your love..? A verdict.
Did you hear.. YOU !! Not Our's…
Until something is ours the sense responsibility takes time to kick in..

And the worst part?

The fear you plant doesn't stay at home.
It travels with us.
It whispers in our exams "Don't mess up again."
It shadows our relationships "You'll disappoint again."
It paces in our careers "You're not enough."

We jump from course to course, job to job, dream to dream.
And sometimes…

we run into wrong arms.. wrong choices.. wrong paths.
Not with ambition… but with panic.
Not with clarity… but with survival.

And then, the invisible cage of values.
The gender bias..!

For boys … excuses.
For girls … expectations.

"Boys will be boys."
"Girls must behave."
Sit properly.. Don't laugh too loud.. Don't dream too much.
Don't wear that..

For girls… a lifetime of shrinking.
For boys… a lifetime of silence.

This is not culture.
This is not tradition.
This is trauma, sugarcoated as "what's right."

And you do it not just with words but with a tone..
That tone.
The one dipped in frustration.
The one soaked in your own unresolved fears.

And then its starts to happen, slowly, silently, heartbreakingly..
They start avoiding you.

My Showdown

I've personally witnessed my kids going through this phase because of tough parenting..
They didn't want to sit at the dining table anymore.
They didn't want to laugh beside us in the living room.
They didn't want to watch TV with us or even attend gatherings where we're present.

Those Lunches..those barbecues…long walks…ice-cream evening..the movie nights…everything is filled with hurt they cant repair.
Not because they hated being around us.
But because our presence has started to feel like a verdict
A courtroom..A firing squad..Not a home..!

And this happens because ..?
They don't feel loved…they feel watched.
They don't feel safe…they feel scrutinised.

And that's not parenting.
That's prison.

So ask yourself..
What have you turned your family time into?

Because if your love feels like a list of failures,
If your concern sounds like commands,
If your guidance feels like a trap…an outburst of your insecurities…your frustrations
Your child will run..

Even if their body stays under your roof,
Their heart will already be gone.
Let this be the moment you shift.
From interrogator to listener.
From judge to gentle guide.
From fear to faith.

Because what your child needs most isn't more pressure.
It's permission.
To breathe…To stumble...To be.

In my experience…
Most of us grew up in households that tested every ounce of our emotional strength.

But once we became parents what happened..?
Where did that empathy go..?
Why repeat what broke us..?

This is not a karmic relay race where pain must be passed down like an heirloom.
Let's not glorify inherited trauma.. Let's end it !!!!!!

Forget those self induced wars within
This is your moment..This is your mirror.
Don't create another cycle.
Don't make your child pay for the silence you were forced to keep.

Don't just wish them peace.. become their peace.

And parents, ask yourselves…

Do you want to raise children who heal from you,
or children who grow because of you..?

Because respect is not demanded.
It is demonstrated.

Love is not earned…It is given.

Your children are not your unfinished business or your second chance in life…
They are their own becoming.

So here is the cry of our soul…
Be our peace, not our pressure.
Be our sanctuary, not our sentence.
Be our roots, not our cage.

Don't just wish us peace … become our peace.

Don't just hand us morals that suffocate.. give us values that liberate.

Don't just raise us to survive.. Raise us to thrive.

Because guilt is not love..And fear is not care.
If your child cannot breathe in your presence…
one day they will choose absence.

The real showdown is not with your children.
It is within you.
Between your fear and your faith.
Between your wounds and your wisdom.
Between the cycle you inherited… and the courage to break it.

So let it end with you.
Let your love not be heavy with judgment but light with acceptance.

Then there comes a moment that cannot be avoided.
It does not announce itself.
It does not demand closure.
The child simply grows old enough to see the pattern without flinching.
To name it without drama.
To realise that understanding is not the same as healing.
Nothing about the past disappears but innocence quietly exits the room.
From that point forward what continues is no longer just inherited..It is participated in.

G^3 Goonj

Your fears, your faith, your wounds, your wisdom all of it lives inside you.
Between the cycle you inherited and the courage to break it lies a choice.

Don't keep revolving around the same traditions and values that once shaped you, scarred you, chained you.

Don't force your children into the same sacrifices that robbed you of joy, the same endless chase for money that left you restless, the same lack of a safe haven that made you grow up too soon.

Create a home where love isn't loud with commands but quiet with acceptance.
Where discipline walks hand-in-hand with dialogue.
Where dreams are not dictated but discovered together

Let it begin now.

Let your love not weigh heavy with judgment but float light with acceptance.

Give this young generation the gift you never received..
a home that heals, not haunts..
a home that strengthens, not suffocates.
Because when children feel safe enough to simply be, they don't just survive… they thrive.
And if money and success matters to you .. explain them to earn a position in life that take cares of everything and help them… guide them to achieve it.. so what if it happens a bit out of the time frame you expected.. the outcome would be marvellous !

And isn't that what you've always wanted to see..your child bloom..?
To see them thrive in ways you once wished for yourself..?

At the end of the day they are your product, your priceless possession, with your traditions and values deep embedded.
Have faith.. Trust them.. Be patient..

They will perform, they will achieve, they will do more than just survive…
Just like you did. Only this time, without carrying the guilt !

There is a stage where awareness stops feeling gentle.
Where insight becomes uncomfortable to carry.

Because once something is seen it cannot be unseen.

My parents shaped the wound.
But they no longer hold authority over its future.
What repeats now does so with my consent.
Not because the pain was imagined.
But because freedom requires ownership.
Healing begins when excuse loses its shelter.

For me understanding my parents did not mean stepping back into the same space that once hurt me.
It meant seeing them clearly while still protecting myself.

From my side the bond was always real and heartfelt and I continued to hold a beautiful relationship with my parents.

Compassion did not require constant closeness.
It asked for honesty about what felt safe and what did not.

Forgiveness did not demand that I shrink or disappear.
It allowed me to remain whole.
I learned that love can exist even with limits and that peace follows when actions come from understanding instead of obligation.
This was not defiance.
This was maturity.

CHAPTER 20

SHOWDOWN WITH TRAPPED EMOTIONS

~THE AFTERLIFE OF UNFELT EMOTION

When the Body Becomes a Diary You Forgot You Were Writing..
For a long time, I believed wounds belonged to the past.

That once an event ended, its authority over me ended too.
That time, distance, maturity, or understanding would naturally loosen its grip.

That belief was comforting and completely untrue.

What body still carries when life moves on..?
Unhealed Wounds…!

Some wounds do not bleed anymore.
They breathe.

They breathe through hesitation.
Through defensiveness that feels reasonable.
Through reactions that arrive faster than choice.
Through fatigue that no amount of rest seems to touch.

We call this personality..We call it temperament.
We call it stress, hormones, bad timing.

But beneath all of that, something older is still active.

Not remembered.. Active..!

When Every Ache is a Sentence and Every Scar a Chapter..
The body does not archive experiences the way the mind does.
It does not label them as past.
It does not file them away neatly with dates and explanations.

It keeps what was unfinished.

Every emotion that did not complete its natural cycle stayed somewhere.
Every moment you had to stay composed while something inside you fractured left a residue.
Every time you swallowed a truth to survive, the body learned to hold it instead.

Not dramatically..Quietly..

This is where trapped emotions live.
This is where unhealed wounds actually reside.

Not in memory but in storage.

There is a common misunderstanding about pain.
We assume the intensity of an experience determines its impact.
That only trauma with a capital T leaves marks.

That is not how it works.

The body is shaped less by what happened and more by what was not allowed to happen afterward.

The cry you stopped.
The anger you redirected inward.
The grief you postponed because there were people depending on you.
The fear you never named because naming it would have changed too much.

Those moments did not dissolve..They settled..like residues

At first, they feel like nothing.
A slight tightness.
A habitual alertness.
A tendency to brace without knowing why.

Later, they begin to speak louder.

Through exhaustion that feels disproportionate.
Through pain that migrates without explanation.
Through patterns that repeat even when you swear you know better now.

This is not punishment.
It is continuity.
The body continuing a conversation the mind walked away from.

I used to think I was strong because I could endure.

I wore endurance like a virtue.
Like proof of evolution.

I could hold space..Hold responsibility..Hold silence.
Hold everyone else together while postponing myself indefinitely.

What I did not realise was that strength without release turns into storage and storage has a cost.

It shows up slowly.
So slowly you learn to negotiate with it.

You adjust your pace.
You adjust your expectations.
You tell yourself this is normal now.

Until one day the body stops negotiating.

My Showdown

I've met the unbearable in hospital corridors.
In a child's confused eyes.
In the absence of people I loved.
In betrayal that still lives in the marrow of my spine.
And in my own mind..when I was afraid of its silence… and more afraid of its noise.

But the loudest encounter..?
When **my body gave up.**

When My Bones Broke and My Soul Cracked Open..

An accident.. Three fractured bones..Three months in bed.
Three lifetimes of emotional unraveling.

People said, "Rest."
But I wasn't resting.
I was being dismantled…cell by cell, memory by memory, identity by identity.

No turning, no lifting, no functioning.
Just existing, horizontal.
The healer couldn't heal herself.

Then one night, under a lazy ceiling fan,
I heard it, not a divine message, not an epiphany.
Just a whisper from somewhere deep
"You're not broken. You're being rewritten."

That's when everything began to shift.
Not externally.. Internally.
The unbearable didn't end but it loosened its grip.

The woman who had always helped others…was now being held by life itself.
And in the deepest stillness, I met myself for the very first time.

Years later it did not announce its rebellion politely.

It arrived as stiffness that did not resolve.
As joints that resisted movement.
As a heaviness that had nothing to do with age and everything to do with accumulation.

Doctors had names for it.
Hormones..Transitions..Natural progression.

They were not wrong..But they were not completely right.

What was happening inside me was not just biological.
It was biographical.

Years of emotional labour without release.
Years of being the one who holds.
Years of staying functional instead of being honest.

My body had become the meeting ground for everything I had not had time to feel.

And it was tired.

The thing about unhealed wounds is this.

When they are not acknowledged, they do not remain passive.
They begin to act.

They influence who feels safe.
What feels threatening.
What feels familiar even when it hurts.

This is how trapped emotion becomes pattern.

The betrayal you never metabolised turns into hyper-vigilance.
The rejection you intellectualised turns into over-giving.
The grief you postponed turns into numbness or fatigue that medicine cannot touch.

We like to believe we are choosing our lives freely.
Often, we are reenacting unresolved chapters with different characters.

Different faces..Same emotional signature.

Not because the universe is cruel but because it is precise.

It keeps bringing you back to the same doorway until you actually walk through it.

Then there is another layer most people do not want to see.

Some wounds are not just carried.. they are preserved.
They become identity.

This is what happened to me.
This is why I am the way I am.
This is what I will never tolerate again.

At some point, the wound stops being an experience and starts being an anchor.

We polish it..We reference it..We protect it.

Not because we enjoy pain.
But because it gives us coherence.

Letting go of a wound often feels like losing the story that explains us.
And without that story, a frightening question waits underneath.

Who am I without this?

This is why healing is resisted even when pain is unbearable.

Because wounds do not just hurt.
They organise identity.

There was a moment in my own life I replayed for years.
A sentence..A silence..A betrayal I never received clarity for.

I carried it quietly.
Used it to justify my mistrust.
Let it colour every relationship that followed.

I told myself I had processed it.
That I was over it.

What I had actually done was constructed tall walls and build a life around it.

One day, a simple question interrupted me.

If that moment does not exist today, its holds no importance today,
why am I still housing it..?

The grief that came then was not for what happened.
It was for the years I gave it my breath.

I did not forget the experience.
I unhooked it.
There is a difference..

Healing does not happen when pain disappears.
It happens when pain stops running the system.

When the body no longer needs to hold guard.
When memory no longer dictates reaction.
When the past is allowed to be complete.

This does not make you soft.
It makes you available.

Available to respond instead of react.
To choose instead of brace.
To live forward instead of sideways.

This is not forgiveness as virtue..tI is hygiene..cleansing..

You are not letting go because anyone else deserves peace.

You are letting go because your system does.

The mistake most people make is thinking healing is an event.

A breakthrough…A conversation…A ritual…A decision.

It is not.!

Healing is a reorientation of relationship.

With the body..With memory..With sensation..
With the pace at which truth is allowed to surface.

What actually changes is not the past.
It is your posture toward it.

When wounds are active, the body stays slightly ahead of the present moment.
It anticipates..It braces..It scans.

Even in joy, something remains watchful.

That vigilance feels intelligent.
It feels earned.
But it is expensive.

The system burns energy protecting you from moments that are no longer happening.
Muscles stay engaged..Breath stays shallow..Sleep stays light..
Pleasure feels conditional.

This is not anxiety.
It is unfinished business running background processes.

At some point, endurance stops being noble.
Not because you are weak.
But because the body has carried enough.

There comes a moment when pain is no longer asking to be managed.

It is asking to be heard.

This is where many people miss the doorway.

They look for solutions instead of signals.
They try to fix the symptom without staying with the sensation long enough to understand it.

Pain is not random..It is specific.

It lives where something was once immobilised.

A voice that went quiet..A movement that was restrained..A truth that was postponed.

The body remembers the moment it had to stop.
And it remembers it precisely.

Grief is often the great unlocker.

Not because it is dramatic.
But because it bypasses control.

When grief arrives fully, it dismantles performance.
It does not ask permission nor respect timing.

It floods the places that has been dry for years.

When my mother died, something fundamental shifted.

The structure that had kept me upright for decades softened.
The role of being strong collapsed without ceremony.

I cried without context.
While cooking..While folding clothes..While finding her handwriting in old notebooks..or notes she wrote me..her recipes..!

The smallest sensory memory could undo me.

And for the first time, I did not stop it.

I did not redirect.
I did not translate it into strength.
I did not make it productive.

I let it move.. and it flowed ..it hustled like a stream falling from hundreds of feet, eager to hit the ground..
An emotional outburst that triggered my immune system..
And I was stuck to my bed for two weeks.

That movement did what years of discipline could not.

It gave my body permission to release what it had been holding on my behalf, for more than a decade.

Not just personal grief.
Ancestral grief..Inherited endurance..
The unspoken agreement to keep going no matter the cost.

What I thought was breaking me was returning me to myself.

Some pain doesn't leave because it has not been completed.

Completion is not understanding..It's an expression.

The body completes experience through movement, sound, breath, tears, rest.

When those are interrupted, the experience stays open.

You do not need elaborate techniques to begin listening again.
You need presence without urgency.

The ability to stay with sensation without immediately explaining it away.
The willingness to feel without deciding what it means.

This is where real steadiness begins.

Not as calm..As capacity..

The capacity to remain present when something uncomfortable arises.
To let the body speak without rushing to silence it.

This is not indulgence.
It is literacy.

Learning the language your system has been using all along.

As wounds loosen, something subtle happens.

Your reactions slow down.
Your breath deepens without effort.
Your body stops rehearsing danger in neutral moments.

You still remember what happened.
But it no longer governs your nervous system.
Memory becomes information instead of instruction.

This is what people mean when they say they feel lighter.

Not because life is easier..or they're healed..
Because they are no longer carrying yesterday into every room.

There is a quiet responsibility that comes with this work.

Not blame but Responsibility.

No one caused your wounds on purpose.
And no one else can release them for you.

But once you see how pain operates inside you, you can no longer unknow it.

You begin to notice when you are armouring instead of responding.
When you are storing instead of feeling.
When you are performing strength instead of allowing support.

This awareness does not make you fragile.
It makes you accurate.

The body does not need perfection.
It needs honesty.

Moments where you stop pushing past sensation and let it register.
Where you choose rest without justification.
Where you allow emotion to move without narrating it.

Healing does not require you to relive everything.
It requires you to stop abandoning yourself when something surfaces.

That is the shift.

G³ Goonj~

What I know now is simple.
My body was never betraying me.
It was keeping score when I could not.

Every ache carried information.
Every fatigue held history.
Every limitation was a message waiting for timing.

The moment I stopped treating pain as an obstacle and started treating it as intelligence, my relationship with myself changed.

Not into softness…Into trust.

I did not erase my wounds just removed their authority.

They stopped deciding how close I could get.
How much rest I was allowed.
How much joy felt safe.

The body relaxed because it was finally being heard.

And when that happened, life did not become perfect.

It became present.

That was enough..!

Your body is not your enemy. It is your first healer.
It has carried everything you were too kind, too strong or too scared to feel.

I once coughed for nearly three months.
Doctors gave me pills, steam, syrups.
I tried yoga, ginger, even a silent retreat.

Nothing worked.

Finally..one day I burst into tears watching an old movie where the mother dies.
I sobbed not just for the movie but for my own mother I had never truly grieved because I was too busy being strong.

That night I slept like a baby..

If you've been reading this and wondering how I speak about wounds with such clarity, how I recognise trapped emotion before it turns into illness, how I understand the body's language when most people are still arguing with it, you're not wrong to wonder.

This understanding did not come from theory.
It came from being inside the wound while it was still open.

From a time when pain was not a concept but a daily reality.
When my body shut down layer by layer.
When I spent months confined to a bed, negotiating with movement, breath, dignity.
When endurance was no longer a choice but a sentence.

The insights you've just read were not learned in hindsight.
They were forged while the wounds were still raw.

In the next chapter, I stop speaking from observation and start speaking from exposure.

Release is not weakness. Release is sacred.
This is your invitation.
This is your showdown.
And this is how your body becomes home again.

That is where the scars appear.
That is where the unbearable enters.
That is where the body's rebellion becomes visible.
That is where the intelligence of pain is no longer explained but lived.

What you've read so far is the understanding that came after survival.
What comes next is the survival itself..

CHAPTER 21

SHOWDOWN WITH THE GENERATIONAL TRAUMA

~WHAT WE INHERIT, WHAT WE INTERRUPT

I grew up in a home where silence had its own language. It wasn't an empty silence. It was layered. Soft at times like the hush of a mother trying not to wake a sleeping child and sometimes sharp like the edge of a father's unspoken disappointments. My earliest memories are stitched with moments that never made it to words. The way my grandmother's eyes would stare blankly into the courtyard after evening prayers as if she was waiting for someone who would never return. The way my mother would hold her breath when the pressure cooker hissed too loudly as though sudden sounds still startled something buried deep in her.

Back then I didn't know these were fragments of their history their own burdens folded into quiet gestures. I thought this was just how families were. Carrying invisible weights like heirlooms passed without ceremony.

Only much later did I realise that what I was calling normal was actually inherited restraint.

When I see how easily today's children label this inheritance it unsettles me. Generational trauma. Two words spoken with rehearsed certainty. Almost like a verdict that ends the conversation before it has even begun.

They say You gave me this wound. It's because of you I am like this.

But I keep wondering. Did we know better. Did they know better.

Did the ones before us have the luxury of pausing mid-survival to study their own pain.

My father worked with his hands until they cracked. He didn't know the language of emotional processing. He knew deadlines hunger responsibility. My mother poured herself into her children into meals cooked with care into prayers whispered before sunrise. She didn't know what boundaries were meant to feel like. She knew how to hold things together.

Did they pass down shadows. Maybe.

But they also passed down something else. Endurance. Continuity. The ability to stand inside difficulty without collapsing.

I remember one monsoon afternoon. I must have been eight or nine. I was digging through my grandfather's old trunk when I found a torn letter folded into itself so many times it had almost become cloth. The ink had faded but the sentence that survived cut through time.

"I am doing this for you. For all of you. So you will not have to see what I have seen."

That day something shifted quietly inside me. I didn't yet have the words for it. But I understood this much. Love does not always arrive as comfort. Sometimes it arrives as absence. Sometimes as silence. Sometimes as a decision made far away from applause.

And yet today children sit across from their parents sometimes still children themselves and say I am broken because of you.

They say it with confidence.. With vocabulary.. With borrowed frameworks that turn life into a neat equation..

But they do not see the nights their parents swallowed tears so they could sleep. They do not see the calculations that happened quietly in kitchens and factories and prayer rooms. They do not see how many versions of themselves their parents abandoned so their children could stand taller.

I ask myself if it is fair.

Fair to tell an ageing mother whose bones now ache under the weight of years that she has handed down pain she never named because she didn't know naming was allowed.

Fair to tell a father whose hands now tremble while lifting a cup of tea that he failed at a skill he was never taught to learn.

There is a part of me that understands repetition. Patterns do travel. Silence echoes. Fear finds new shapes.

But I have also noticed something else.

I have caught myself pausing mid-sentence because my voice suddenly sounded like my mother's. I have felt my body choose quiet when speaking would have been easier. I have withheld softness without knowing why not out of cruelty but out of habit.

That was the moment it became undeniable.

Inheritance is not something we accuse others of. It is something we discover ourselves inside of.

When I look at my parents now I don't see just their mistakes. I see a chain of human beings responding to life as it came to them. I see parents shaped by scarcity by fear by responsibilities that arrived before readiness.

My grandmother once said to me so softly I almost missed it We didn't know life was allowed to be easy.

That sentence lives in my body.

Because maybe that is the real lineage. Not trauma alone. But effort. Adjustment. Incremental hope.

Each generation trying to loosen the knot a little more than the one before.

Yes there may be something called generational trauma. It may whisper through habits and live in unspoken reflexes.

But there is also generational love. The kind that does not announce itself. The kind that works overtime without credit. The kind that keeps showing up even when language fails.

And somewhere between what we received and what we choose not to repeat there is agency.

So when I think of children standing across from their parents with accusation in their eyes I want to say this gently.

Ask before you indict. Listen before you conclude.

Remember that the people who raised you were once children too. Raised by someone else's fear someone else's limits someone else's unfinished healing.

Do not turn your newfound awareness into a weapon. Awareness is meant to widen compassion not sharpen blame.

Because one day the vocabulary will change again.

One day your children will sit across from you holding words you do not yet understand. Frameworks you did not grow up with. Expectations you never rehearsed.

And when that day comes you will hope they remember one thing.

That you were not perfect.

That you were learning in real time.

That you were human too.

Before I could question anyone else life found a way to corner me first.
Not through memory.
Through reaction.

My Showdown

My real confrontation with generational trauma did not happen in a conversation with my parents.
It happened in a moment when no one else was in the room.

I was already grown. Already articulate. Already armed with awareness.
And yet there I was standing in my own kitchen reacting far more intensely than the moment required.

Nothing dramatic had happened.
A small misunderstanding. A tone. A pause.

But my body responded as if history had just walked back in.

My jaw tightened before my mind could intervene. My breath shortened and silence rushed in faster than thought.

And suddenly I recognised it.

This was not a wound being given to me.
This was a reflex I had been carrying.

Not consciously chosen.
Not consciously learned.
But rehearsed over years of watching how restraint survived.

That was my showdown.

Not with my parents.

Not with their choices.
But with the part of me that wanted healing without responsibility.

In that moment I saw the trap clearly.

Blame is easier than ownership.
Understanding is easier than interruption.
Naming a pattern is easier than stopping it mid-breath.

I could trace the lineage perfectly.
But tracing did not absolve me from choice.

That night I didn't call anyone.
I didn't journal.
I didn't spiritualise it.

I simply sat with the uncomfortable truth that healing was no longer about what I inherited.
It was about what I was willing to carry forward.

That was the day generational trauma stopped being a concept for me.
And became a mirror.

G³ GOONJ ~

There is a quiet arrogance hiding inside modern healing.
The belief that awareness alone makes us exempt.

It doesn't.
Awareness does not absolve us. It makes us responsible.

Your parents may have passed things down unconsciously.
The moment you see it it becomes conscious.
And from that moment on the lineage runs through you.

Healing is not about indicting the past.
It is about deciding what ends with you without needing applause for it.

You are allowed to acknowledge pain without turning it into a courtroom.
You are allowed to want better without erasing what kept you alive.

And one day when you are tired in ways you never predicted
when your children misunderstand you using language you never learned
you will realise something quietly humbling.

Every generation heals blindfolded.
With limited tools.
Inside real life.

So if there is one thing worth passing down
let it not be perfection.

Let it be humility.

The humility to say
I did not know everything.
But I tried to loosen the knot.

That is not trauma.
That is transmission with conscience.

And that is enough.

CHAPTER 22

SHOWDOWN WITH THE SHADOW

~THIRTY YEARS UNDER ANOTHER'S LIGHT

The longer you live under someone's shadow, the harder it becomes to cast your own.

There are people whose presence feels like sunlight. Warm, steady, protective.
You lean toward them. You grow under their gaze. You begin to believe that their brightness is safety.
And maybe it is, in the beginning.

Until the day you realise the light isn't shining on you.
It's shining through you.
And you've long stopped existing as anything but a reflection.

That's when the real shadow begins.
Not the kind that follows you.
The kind that hovers over you.

The kind that teaches you to check yourself before you speak.

Not consciously. Not deliberately.
Just a brief glance. A flicker of the eyes.
As if some internal calibration needs to happen first.

The Light That Never Learned to ..Shine
They came into my life during a storm, when everything I had was collapsing.

They helped me.. Guided me.. Lifted me out of chaos..

They made me feel protected, seen, understood.

For someone who had always fought alone, that kind of safety felt divine.

In the beginning, it was rescue.
Later, it became routine.
And eventually, it turned into rule.

They decided what I should wear, what I should pursue, how I should speak, what was appropriate and what wasn't.
It was never said outright. The control was wrapped in wisdom.
It sounded like concern. It sounded like experience.

It sounded like, Trust me. I know better.

And I believed them.

Because when someone saves you, you start believing they have earned the right to define what saving looks like.

So I adjusted.
Softened.
Learned the rhythm of agreement.

Before answering questions, I would glance at them.
Not for permission.
More like alignment.

As if my words needed to pass through another filter before they were allowed into the room.

The Gradual Disappearance

Years passed, and I became fluent in silence.

I stopped voicing my opinions because they would either be corrected or quietly overwritten.

I stopped celebrating my achievements because they somehow became shared property.
Even my emotions were moderated. What was too loud. Too soft. Too dramatic. Too detached.

It was easier to adapt than to argue.
Easier to obey than to offend.
Easier to disappear than to be disapproved of.

You don't notice when it happens.
How dependency starts looking like devotion.
How fear starts dressing itself up as loyalty.

How peace begins to feel conditional.

Every attempt to stretch was met not with resistance, but with familiarity.
A gentle reminder of who I was supposed to be.

And each time, without realising it, I checked myself again.
That small glance..That internal pause.

The Awakening

It wasn't an explosion.
It was a whisper.

We were surrounded by people. The same circle that always revolved around them.
They were speaking, commanding, impressing.
I was smiling on cue, as always.

Someone asked me something. About my work. My life.

Before I could answer, they answered for me.

Laughter followed.
And I laughed too. Because that's what I had trained myself to do.

But something cracked open.

For the first time, I wasn't laughing with them.
I was laughing at myself.

That night, I stood in front of the mirror and couldn't recognize the woman looking back.
Every choice calibrated. Every emotion measured. Every instinct second-guessed.

I realised I had been living as a reflection for so long that I had forgotten the sensation of being a source.

It wasn't love anymore.
It was worship.

And I was the offering.

That's when it landed with clarity sharp enough to cut:

The longer you live under someone's shadow, the harder it becomes to cast your own.

The Showdown

For years, I told myself I couldn't walk away.
Not out of fear. Out of gratitude.

They had stood by me in my worst storms.
Helped my family. Carried burdens. Paid bills. Held structures together.

How do you rebel against someone who once rescued you?

But here is the truth no one prepares you for:

Even a saviour can become your jailer if the debt never ends.

And gratitude, when stretched beyond its season, curdles into guilt.

So I didn't break the rules.
I broke the pattern.

Quietly.

I started earning, not for status, but for sovereignty.
I stopped seeking approval before speaking.
I made decisions without rehearsing how they would be received.

And one day, something small happened.

I answered a question without looking first.

No glance..No internal check..No calibration.

I realised it afterward.

Nothing collapsed..No storm followed..No punishment arrived.

Only space.

That's when I noticed the shadow shrinking.
Not because I fought it.
But because I had stepped out from beneath it.
Only then did I see it clearly.

Not a parent..Not a mentor..Not a guardian.

A spouse.

Three decades of shared life where love had quietly mutated into dominance and devotion into debt.

It wasn't cruelty.
It was conditioning.
Perfected over time.. Polished with affection..
Cemented with obligation.

You can live beside someone for a lifetime and still never meet yourself.

The Reclamation

So how do you fix something like this without tearing down the roof you've lived under for thirty years?

You fix you.

Not loudly.. Not rebelliously.. Not theatrically.

You stop waiting to be chosen.
You stop negotiating for worth.
You stop explaining your light to those who fear its glare.

You detach emotionally, not physically.
You build a room inside your mind that no one else has access to.

You stay, but you no longer serve.
You love, but you no longer disappear.
You coexist as your own entity. Equal. Silent. Sovereign.

Not everything becomes easier.
Some warmth fades.
Some familiarity cools.

But what you gain is something far rarer.

Yourself..!

G³ GOONJ ~

The longer you live under someone's shadow, the harder it becomes to cast your own.
But once you remember your light was never theirs to manage or measure,
you stop living as reflection and start burning as source.

This is not anger.
Not escape.
But a quiet, absolute reclaiming of power.

And the most dangerous thing about rediscovering your light?
You no longer need permission to exist.

What they never tell you is this:
The shadow usually knows exactly what it's doing.

It isn't accidental.
It measures your movements, your moods, your momentum.
It ensures you never rise high enough to outgrow its reach.

And when confronted, it hides behind nobility of intent.

He still believes he did what was best.
Best for me.
Best for the people around us.
Best for the world he built.

There is no remorse. Only righteousness.
A cold certainty that control was care, restraint was protection, dominance was destiny.

That's how superiority feeds itself.
By convincing the world its light is benevolence, not blindness.

But here is the truth.

Even the most imposing shadow cannot exist without a stronger light behind it.

And that light was always mine.

So I don't curse the shadow.
I outgrow it.

Because once you remember your own brilliance,
no man's conviction, no matter how righteous,
can eclipse your soul again.

She wasn't destroyed.
Just momentarily eclipsed.

CHAPTER 23

SHOWDOWN WITH FEAR

~WHEN THE FIRE BECAME THE PRAYER

There was a time when fear quietly ruled my life.
Not the obvious kind of fear.. the one that makes you jump or run but the subtle, creeping kind.
The fear of not being good enough. The fear of being rejected. The fear of failing. It disguised itself as self-doubt, hesitation, and endless "if's and but's." And I didn't even realise it was rooted in how I saw myself or rather, how I didn't see myself.
It wasn't society that held me back. Not really. It was my own belief that I had to meet certain expectations, fit certain moulds, and ignore the voice within. I was abiding by rules I never agreed to, following standards that never truly belonged to me.
What I didn't know then is that the more I ignored myself..my feelings, my body, my voice..
the more I fed that fear, slowly, it started eating away..
my confidence.. my joy.. my mental peace.

A point came in my life when I realised I had been neglecting the most important relationship in my life.. the one with myself. I had been chasing validation from the outside while my inner world was collapsing. I had forgotten that my strength, my creativity, my ability to grow all of it depended on how I related to me.
To face the world, to take on the challenges of life, to truly live I first needed to embrace my whole self.
My strengths, yes, but also my flaws.

My quirks.. My shadows..
The parts of me that I thought made me unworthy… they were actually what made me real.
Those what if's and but what about… thoughts I used to dismiss? I started to see them as signals. They weren't signs of weakness. They were signs that I needed to pay attention.
They showed up whenever I was afraid to try, afraid to be judged, afraid to fall. And every time they appeared,
I had a choice.. listen with compassion, or silence them with criticism.
I began choosing compassion. And from that space, I started healing. I learned that I'm not just a mind, or a body, or a bundle of feeling..
I'm all of it.. interconnected, layered, evolving..
a living system of breath, memory, scars, wisdom, and spirit.
There's a physical part of me that gets tired, sore, or sluggish and needs care.
There's an emotional part of me that carries joy, sadness, fear, and hope and all those feelings are valid.
There's the intellectual me, curious and hungry for knowledge.
There's the social side of me that craves connection and healthy relationships.
And then, there's the spiritual part.. the one that asks bigger questions, seeks meaning, and longs for peace.
I'm NOT One-Dimensional and Neither Are You

And to heal, I had to learn to care for every layer of my being.
To pause when my body whispered.
To soothe when emotions surged.
To seek meaning when everything felt pointless.
To know that my wholeness wasn't a destination. It was a daily remembering.
To truly take care of myself.. I had to learn to tune in to all these layers. That's when balance started to return.

I began with the simplest things.
I noticed the way my body reacted in certain situations..tightness in my chest, a sinking feeling in my stomach, tension in my back. These weren't random. They were messages from within.
Whenever I felt uneasy around someone, I gave myself permission to set boundaries. When I felt drained, I stopped pushing through and let myself rest. I paid attention to what made me feel lighter, calmer, and more myself.
Mindful breathing became a tool. Just placing my hand on my diaphragm and slowing down my breath helped me return to the present moment. That moment of pause gave me clarity.
On days when I felt numb or disconnected, I reached out to a friend. When the noise in my mind got too loud, I took walks in nature or wrote pages after pages to empty my thoughts.
I even gave myself small treats, a massage, a hot bag on my back, a favourite snack anything that whispered, "You matter..!"

Now..what you are about to read is not about fear.. it is about what rises when fear collapses.
If these pages tremble in your hands, it is because they are alive.
This is the most spiritual experience I have ever survived.
Step in carefully.. The dance is still echoing..

The air was molten that afternoon the kind that makes silence crackle.
I stood at the edge of the terrace, sweat glints on my skin like small shards of glass.. my heartbeat louder than the city below.
The sun glared without mercy..the tiles beneath my feet were burning hot, but I stayed.
Because I had run out of places to run.
The mantras were already playing…this was my daily ritual… but the moment the first drumbeat of this one mantra struck…it was like thunder rolling through my spine. Not that I had never

heard this before, it was my playlist.. but the intensity of it had suddenly aligned with my present..
My palms trembled, my breath staggered, but something ancient inside me began to rise.
Not courage..!
something deeper..Something older than fear itself..

The sound swelled.. The air thickened.. The world vanished..
And I.. a wife, a mother, a healer, a woman who had spent a lifetime bowing to fear lifted my arms to the blazing sky. Tears rolling down mixed with the trickling sweat and there was movement… I was moving… I before I could even realise…

The dance began.

There was a time when fear quietly ruled my life.
Not the kind that startles you into a sprint but the kind that sneaks in with good manners, smiles politely, and rearranges your insides while you're too tired to notice.
It spoke like caution, behaved like humility, dressed up as obedience.
I let it stay because it looked so responsible so respectable
I thought it was protecting me from mistakes.
But really.. it was protecting me from myself.

Every harsh tone, every careless word, every slammed door in the house became evidence that I was somehow wrong, somehow less.
Someone's temper wasn't even mine to carry yet I wore it.
Every raised voice felt like punishment…every silence, rejection.
And I let it eat through me quietly, all of it, bit by bit,
my confidence, my laughter, my peace.. bit by silent bite.

Fear fed on my guilt.
It fed on my habit of keeping the peace at the cost of my truth.
It fed on my constant apology for existing.

It fed until I no longer knew what I wanted..only what would keep others comfortable.

And when life decided to test every nerve, it fed more greedily.
Health began to falter.. Money grew tight..
Banks began clawing back loans..
Responsibilities multiplied..
Every problem arrived together, a stampede of demands and I stood in the middle trying to breathe.

It felt like a boulder rolling down from the cliff above
and I was right in its path.. too frozen to move.. too tired to think.. too loyal to scream..
Fear had become my geography.
I didn't just feel afraid.. I lived in fear..!

Nights were sleepless, long and breathless.
The ceiling fan turned slow circles above me while blades of my mind spun faster inside.
Every thought was a spiral..,What if this doesn't end? What if I fail? What if I lose everything?
Anxiety came in waves that left salt in my veins.
And yet, one evening, amid the exhaustion, a small voice.. the kind that doesn't come from logic..whispered,
Move.. Not run.
Not escape.. Move.
Sweat it out.
It was instinct more than inspiration.
As a creative soul, I had always believed that movement was medicine.
The body remembers what the mind cannot say.
Little did I know.. that day, my body demanded an exorcism.
Fierce as fury !

The air trembled

The sun had lowered but the heat hadn't. I climbed to the terrace, barefoot, carrying every unshed tear in my bones.
The city felt distant..only the wind and the mantras remained.

And then the incantation of Shiv Tandav stotram..
The drum.. The roar.. The invocation..
(To resonate with what I felt...play the Shiv Tandav stotram in the background and continue reading)

Because I was drowning... and when you are drowning in fear, you do not need a gentle god.
You need one who burns everything false.
You need Shiva ! the destroyer of illusion, the purifier of poison, the one who dances in the middle of death and still creates life.

The first beat hit, and my body answered.
At first slow, awkward... what am I doing.. what if someone watches me they'll think I've lost it.. then came a jolt that shook me from inside..heart palpitating at its peak...trembling...then faster, fiercer, unstoppable.
Every stomp was defiance.. Every spin was surrender..
Every breath turned into chant.

I wasn't dancing to look divine, I was dancing to become divine.. to give my fear somewhere else to go.

The floor scorched my soles, but the heat inside me was wilder.
The mantras intensity grew louder, filling the evening with something primal, something ancient.
My tears mixed with sweat...my pain turned to rhythm.
And in that madness, fear finally stopped being the enemy and became my fuel.

I realised Shiva was not in the sky.
He was in the pulse of my wrists.
He was in the cracking of my voice.

He was the witness, and the witnesser, and the fire between the two.
I kept moving until the mind broke open..until the exhaustion gave way to emptiness and emptiness gave way to presence.

It wasn't peace it was clarity
A stillness so fierce that it silenced every "what if" that had ever haunted me.
And this form of dancing became my sacred ritual !

That day, I did not defeat fear.
I simply stopped letting it sit on my throne.
I saw it for what it was…a shadow that could not exist without my light.

Fear will always visit..But will only stay where it is worshipped.
You do not owe fear your loyalty, your obedience or your silence.
You do not owe it your throne..the sacred seat of your spirit.
Because once you remember who you are..the pulse behind the breath, the rhythm inside the storm, you realise something extraordinary.

Fear does not bow to courage..It bows to awareness.
And when awareness dances, fear kneels.

You are not here to escape fear. You are here to burn through it, to turn it into movement, to turn movement into prayer..into the most scared ritual that ever existed

So when fear arrives again.. and it will..
don't freeze.. Don't shrink.. Don't run..

Step forward.. let the ground scorch.
Let the sweat trickle and bite.. just remember
You are not the one who trembles before fear.
You are the one before whom fear trembles.
You are the Tandav..!

CHAPTER 24

SHOWDOWN WITH THE FIRE THAT NEVER TOUCHED ME

~YOU CANNOT BE TOUCHED BY WHAT YOU REFUSE TO CARRY

Hatred is an endless circle of fear and desperation.
But even as a child, I somehow stood outside that circle.

And inside the chapter as core revelations most people never dare to look at

People ask what came first...
fear, hypocrisy, insecurity, the need to protect their own egos, or the desperation to feel superior to someone, anyone.
I watched people spiral in and out of hatred with such ease that it almost looked like a reflex.
But inside me?
That reflex never existed.

I need to make one thing absolutely clear, if not for anyone else, then for my own soul.
Hatred was never mine. I wasn't born with it, I wasn't raised around it, and I never learned it.
Through childhood chaos, schoolyard cruelty, college politics, bullies wearing uniforms and bullies wearing friendships, extended family dramas and the quiet wars people fight inside their own homes, I kept discovering the same thing..

I am made of a different clay. I could be intimidated..
yes. I could compare myself..
yes. I could carry grudges about not feeling enough..
yes. But I never crossed into hatred, not even once.
Not in thought, not in intention, not in revenge.
I never sabotaged, never competed to destroy, never shunned someone just to feel taller.
That darkness doesn't live in me. And I say this without hypocrisy or a halo..
I say it because it is the truth of my entire life. I have survived too much to lie about who I am.

So when life pushed me, when pain matured me, when people disappointed me, when betrayal walked too close,
when insecurity poisoned the air I breathed, I still could not hate.
I processed..I cried..I questioned.
I resented..I broke..I healed.
But I never hated.

And then came marriage.
A different battlefield.
A different curriculum.
A different karma.

Despite those arguments and issues in my married life, I never developed hatred for my spouse.
He was also insecure of losing me and his love, fear, confusion all of it made him act in ways neither of us understood then.
But even in the worst moments, he never hated me and somewhere deep inside, something in him always knew me.

I knew the law of karma too intimately to let my heart rot with bitterness.
I understood that my soul also carried its own karmic burden.
Running away from the decision the universe placed in my destiny would only delay the cleansing my spirit needed.

These people, these challenges, this marriage, this journey they're all shaping me, grinding me, purifying me.
So yes, I resented my life for a few long years but I never abandoned it.

That resentment didn't come from hatred.
It came from unawareness.
From not yet understanding the architecture of karma.
From not knowing that the person hurting me was also living inside the pressure of his own karmic script.

The law doesn't isolate pain.
If you're the victim in one moment, you may also be the initiator of another karmic domino that shapes someone else's destiny.
We are all woven into each other's timelines.

Once I understood this, resentment dissolved too.
Otherwise..why else would I be so cordial to the ones who tested me ?

I met every challenge head-on… Even the people who hurt me beyond words and trust me,
there is a book in me for that chapter too.. I could never hate them. Maybe I felt intimidated. Maybe I felt "less than."
Maybe I held grudges about not feeling enough.
But Never. Hated..never Sabotage? Never. Revenge? Never.
What I speak here is not self-polishing.. it is truth. If anyone thinks this is the extent of my suffering,
then they know nothing about my life.

And because hatred never took root inside me, I learned the most transformative truth of all..
you cannot be touched by what you refuse to carry.

People project hatred because they cannot digest their own insecurities.

People pass down bitterness because nobody taught them a healthier inheritance.
People hate easily because the alternative introspection is too heavy for them to hold.

But I was never built for hatred.
I was built for awareness.
For karmic endurance.
For emotional transmutation.
For spiritual rebellion.
For survival without bitterness.

In short, I was a warrior…
not the kind who fights battles outside,
but the kind who walks into the fire within and returns with her soul intact.
The kind who bleeds truth instead of vengeance.
The kind who knows that every wound is a doorway and every betrayal is a training ground.

I was a warrior who learned to stand still when the world wanted me shattered,
to choose consciousness over chaos, to choose alignment over approval,
to choose elevation over reaction.

A warrior who realised that awakening is not a moment…
it is a lifetime of choosing yourself even when your past tries to pull you back into darkness.

A warrior forged in showdowns, shaped by karma, humbled by pain,
but resurrected by truth.

And that is why my story is not a tale of suffering…
its a scripture of strength.

Every chapter, every fracture, every falling-apart became the exact initiation needed
to become who I was always destined to be..

A spiritual warrior..who fights none, but transforms all.

Some souls come into this world to break patterns.
Some come to end generational cycles.
Some come to burn the poison without becoming poisonous.

I am one of those souls.
I burn… but I don't become ash.
I break… but I don't break others.
I hurt… but I don't contaminate.

I walk through fire and come out with clarity, not cruelty.

Maybe that is why the Divine tests certain people more.
Because only certain souls can go through hell and still refuse to hate the ones who pushed them into the flames.

Hatred never belonged to me.
And I never belonged to hatred.
My path was purification, not retaliation.

And the truth is, everyone can break this cycle.
But only when they stop asking, "Why is this happening to me?"
And start asking, "What is this trying to free me from?"

I was freed from hatred without ever touching it.
I was freed from resentment by understanding it.
I was freed from the karmic maze by walking through it.
And I was freed from pain by accepting that every soul is living its own karmic exam
and mine simply demanded a higher syllabus.

I survived without hating.
I healed without hardening.

I grew without destroying.
I learned without avenging.

And that is the real showdown.
Not with hatred.
But with everything inside me that tried to make room for it and failed.

My showdown

This is the part people never see.
Everyone sees the healed woman.
Nobody sees the battlefield she crawled through.

My showdown was never against another human being.
My showdown was with the parts of me that could have easily turned bitter, easily turned revengeful,
easily turned hateful… but never did.

My showdown was with silence.
With swallowing pain without understanding why.
With living in a house where arguments had their own seasons.
With a life that asked too much from a girl who had barely learned to breathe.
With situations where dignity was questioned, strength was tested, faith was squeezed between ribs.

My showdown was with the version of me who kept getting up even when there was nothing left to rise from.

And the biggest showdown of all was this…
learning to see people through the lens of their karma.. instead of the lens of my pain.

Once that clicked, everything else changed.

I stopped personalising their actions.
I stopped taking their wounds as my worth.

I stopped thinking I was the target.
And I stopped expecting fairness from people whose karmic cycles were in chaos.

The moment I understood karma, the enemy disappeared.
There was no one to hate.
No one to punish.
No one to blame.
Only souls, all equally confused, equally wounded, equally entangled in their own karmic necessities.

From that moment, hatred had no space in me.
Not because I forgave.
But because I understood.
And understanding is stronger than forgiveness.
Understanding dissolves the wound instead of covering it.

This was my showdown !
choosing clarity over cruelty, choosing awareness over anger, choosing wisdom over war.

People speak of karma with too much confidence…
as if they have seen the threads, touched the equations, read the divine script.
In truth, most people use the word "karma" the way angry people use stones…
to throw, to accuse, to justify hatred.

In 2020, when Nirmal lay in a hospital bed fighting for breath,
when 95 percent of his lungs surrendered to a virus,
when three months felt like a lifetime stretched thin, a close friend said to me
"This is karma, Gunjan.
His payback.
Just like you were hospitalised for three months…now he is too.
The universe is settling the score."

He said it casually, sarcastically.
But it hit me with the weight of something sacred being mishandled.

For a moment, the world became absolutely still.
Not silent still.
As if the truth itself paused to watch what I would do with that sentence.

Because here's the thing no one knew..
If I had carried even a drop of hatred for him, that statement would have fed it.
It would have justified it.
It would have validated the bitterness I had every right to feel.

But I didn't hate him.
Not then.
Not even when life pushed me to the edge.
How could I ? … I was made to love ..made to understand…

That's the part people never understood.
That's the part even the universe paused to witness.

I could have weaponised karma.
I could have worn my suffering like evidence.
I could have claimed the throne of victimhood.
But hatred never found a home inside me.

And it wasn't because I was divine or saintly.
It was because hating him would have made me exactly what pain wanted me to become.

A mirror of the wound.
A reflection of the hurt.
Another link in the chain of inherited bitterness.

Instead, I saw something else..

His suffering wasn't revenge.
It wasn't repayment.
It wasn't "my turn to watch him break."

It was his karmic crossing.
His soul's examination.
His moment of being stripped down to the roots of himself.

Karma wasn't punishing him.
Karma was positioning him.
Just like it had positioned me years ago.

Karma was giving him one more opportunity to do things right..!

He wasn't spared by chance.
He wasn't saved by medicine alone.
He wasn't saved my prayers.
He wasn't breathing because the universe forgot to settle its debts.

He was breathing because his soul had been granted a second window..
a second chance to rise above his own shadow,
a chance to soften where he had hardened,
a chance to feel what he had once ignored,
a chance to understand life, love, fragility… and me.

He wasn't saved to suffer.
He was saved so he could shift..

So he could make right what life had quietly been asking him to repair.
So he could rewrite the patterns he had inherited.
So he could finally meet the weight of his own heart not as a man who survived a virus..
but as a man who survived himself.

Everyone talked about karma like it was retribution.
But I saw something else entirely.

This was grace disguised as consequence.
Mercy disguised as illness.
A cosmic pause button giving him one last chance to realign.

Not to repay me.
Not to apologise.
Not to balance a ledger.

But to evolve..
He was saved not to stay the same…
but saved so he could finally, fully, consciously…To make it right
!

The hatred others expected me to carry…
I simply refused.

Because hatred would have bound me to the past.
It would have kept me trapped in a version of myself I had already outgrown.
It would have made me smaller, harder, darker.

But I had already walked through my fire.
I had already tasted awakening.
I had already learned the secret..

The fire that burns you is not the fire that transforms you.
The fire that transforms you is the one you refuse to throw at someone else.. GGG

Watching Nirmal suffer was not satisfaction.
It was not closure.
It was not karmic symmetry.

It was a reminder that every soul has its own path, its own lessons, its own moment of collapse.

The fire that should have burned me into bitterness but somehow purified me instead.
My power was not in surviving the situation, it was in refusing to hate the man who unintentionally wounded me,
only to accept the universal law.

And I, despite everything, was not meant to hate him.
I was meant to witness him.
To rise beside him.
To evolve through him.

His sickness cracked me open.
My fractures woke him up.
But hatred never touched us.
And that is why we survived.

Through those cracks…we didn't break apart.
We rebuilt.
We softened.
We matured.
We became an example for our children that some battles are won through silence, dignity,
and choosing not to poison your own heart.

I didn't rise from the fall.
I rose from the fire I refused to ignite.
That fire…the one I could've used to burn everything down…
that never touched me.

And that, truly, was my showdown.

G³ Goonj ~

People often ask, "Why do some people hate so easily? Why do they hurt without thinking?"
The answer is simple and merciless… because their karma is playing out.

Some souls fall into hatred like it is gravity , not because they are evil but because their evolution has not begun.
They are looped inside their own karmic cycle, repeating actions their soul was begging them to rise above.
Not because nobody warned them… but because they ignored every warning.

The deeper meaning is…
Karma is architectural.
It is engineering..It is sequencing..It is timeline mathematics..

You are not suffering randomly..Nobody is..

When someone hurts you, two karmas activate simultaneously:
1- Your karma of receiving that experience
2-Their karma of creating that experience

These two karmas collide in the same timeline but they do not come from the same origin.
They simply meet each other to complete a lesson.

You may be the wounded one in the scene but you may also be the trigger for their karmic fall,
karmic awakening, karmic test or karmic reward.

This is why hatred is pointless as It misunderstands the architecture of destiny.

The person hurting you may not be acting from choice.
They may be acting from compulsion.
A karmic compulsion.!!
Something they cannot escape until the lesson is completed.

And your presence in their life may be the catalyst that pushes them toward that completion.

This is why my heart never learned hatred.

Because I was blessed with awareness to see the bigger map.

I saw that karma is not "you versus me."

Karma is...
"soul versus self."
"Ego versus truth."
"Patterns versus evolution."
"Destiny versus denial."

When I realised this..everything softened.

The husband who hurt me had his karma.
I had mine.
We met each other's karma.
We shaped each other's evolution.
We pushed each other toward maturity.

Some karma heals your past.
Some karma breaks you.
Some karma builds you.
Some karma refines you.
Some karma prepares your future.
Some karma clarifies your soul's rank.

And some karma is placed solely to ensure you never become the person who hurt you.

That was my karma.
To endure without absorbing.
To feel without collapsing.
To walk through fire without becoming fire.

When hatred does not grow inside you, it means your soul is being trained for a different level of spiritual responsibility.
A different curriculum... A higher syllabus... A cleaner destiny..

The Divine knows who can carry darkness without becoming dark.
I was one of them.

And that is the real karmic victory.
Not that I survived what happened to me.
But that I never became what happened to me.

And here's the truth..
every single person who hates, hurts, manipulates, humiliates or destroys…
was given a chance not to.

Their intuition whispered..Their conscience tugged.
Their inner Shalya screamed at them from the inside..
Don't do this. Don't hurt this person. Don't betray this soul.
Don't put yourself first at someone else's cost.
Don't choose ego. Don't choose cruelty. Don't wound what the Divine sent into your life for a reason.

The voice was there..
The signals were there..
The divine interventions were there..

But they refused to listen.

Why?
Because their karma demanded expression.
Their choices were the evidence.
Their actions were the exam.
And their downfall, awakening or transformation will depend entirely on..
how they handled the soul standing in front of them.

What they did to you was never about your worth.
It was always the unfolding of their karmic script, a timeline of their own downfall.

A karmic loop they must complete, even if it means breaking themselves on the way.

My task was never to hate them.
My job was to witness their karma without letting it contaminate mine or adding any new karmic burden onto my own.

And for that…I am deeply… fiercely grateful..!
Grateful to every divine energy, every unseen intervention, every moment of whispered awareness that saved
me from reacting, saved me from adding more karma, saved me from becoming someone my soul would regret.
Grateful for the enlightenment that held my hand when my humanity was shaking.

I'm sure… by now you understand something most people spend lifetimes failing to see…
why someone cheats you, why someone backstabs you, why someone manipulates you,
why someone behaves in ways that bruise your soul.
It is never just their flaw or their choice.
It is your karma and their karma colliding at the exact divine timing meant to awaken you both.
Two karmic scripts playing out simultaneously
one exposing them, one evolving you.

You cannot control the timing.
You cannot edit their chapter.
You can only choose how cleanly you exit yours.

From this understanding comes a sacred power
the power to break the cycle of hatred.
And yes, you can.
You just have to become the balance between pain and peace.. between reaction and realisation.

Instead of pitting one part of yourself against the other, the hurt against the healer,
the anger against the awareness…align them.

Because the truth is… the answer always lies in the balance.
That is where hatred dissolves and karma transforms.

And sometimes, the deepest balance is knowing when a karmic cycle is ending.
There comes a moment…quiet, unmistakable…when your soul knows something your mind cannot articulate..
This script is complete..!

This is not the karma you need to keep suffering through to be "good" in the next life.
This is the karma you need to walk away from to be whole in this one.

Recognising that moment is a higher intelligence of the soul a sacred sixth sense
that tells you..
You have learned what you came here to learn.
Staying will only bend you, not build you.
Leaving will not create more karma…
it will close the chapter with grace.

Yes, if you are strong enough, you can outgrow the pain by living through it.
But if you are wise enough, you can end the cycle by stepping out of it.

Because karmic liberation is not only about endurance..
it is about clarity.
It is the courage to stay when your soul is learning and the courage to leave when your soul is done.

That is where destiny shifts.

That is where patterns break.
That is where karma finally bows down to consciousness.

With this truth, this chapter closes like a door behind me…
and another one opens into the next showdown.

CHAPTER 25

SHOWDOWN WITH POWER

~WHEN SOMETHING TRUER TAKES THE THRONE

Redefining Power: A Soul's Unraveling..
Once, it wore heels that never stumbled. It spoke with sharp certainty, never cracking, never crying.
It looked like perfection stitched tight, unshakable, untouchable, always composed.

I chased that version.
I performed it.
And still, I broke inside it.

But now…?
Now, power is the quietest thing I know.
It's not something I wear.
It's the moment I choose to take the damn mask off.

It looks like knowing when to walk away not out of weakness, but out of respect for my peace.
It's the even braver act of staying, not because I'm scared to leave but because my soul whispered,
"This matters."
It's in the soft rebellion of trusting my 'yes' without needing permission.
And the holy defiance of trusting my no without explaining why.
"I will no longer betray myself even if it makes others uncomfortable."
It's not about fighting, yelling or proving a point.

It's not rebellion from ego.. it's rebellion from truth.
It's choosing you, your peace, your values, your voice, over fitting into roles that shrink you.

Power isn't loud anymore. It's anchored..!
It's rooted in truth, not control.
It no longer shouts to be heard, it whispers and is still obeyed.
Like..

There was a time in my life when I didn't even realise how much of myself I had handed over.
Not just to a system, not just to society, family , friends, my parents and majorly to someone I deeply revered as my spiritual mother.
She is my guide, my guru, my Maa, my anchor. I see her as the divine walking among us. And in serving her, I was serving the Divine. So I gave her everything.. my time, my energy, my presence.

For nearly 17 years, I stood beside her not just in faith but in service. Every festival, every ritual, every prayer, I was there.
Her trust in me was complete and mine in her was unwavering.
And for that, I am and will always be grateful.
Her love for me is boundless and she has supported me in ways no one else did. Just her presence gave me emotional strength.
From the difficult phases to offering financial and mental support when I needed it most.
My pain moved her. She saw me. Cared for me. Held space for me when the world didn't.
And I gave myself to the seva fully, wholeheartedly.
It was not a duty .... I was the chosen one.. it was a joy. A privilege.
A blessing I cherished.
But what no one saw, and what even I didn't fully acknowledge for a long time was the toll it quietly took on me.

I was Torn Between Devotion and Drowning..

Despite my challenges and struggles on a personal front.. I kept myself available all the time. Whatever I was doing at work, at home, in my personal life.. I would drop everything to be there for her. She had grown to rely on me and I never let her down.

But behind the scenes, my life was unraveling.
My work life was a battle.
My family life was fragile.
My emotional and mental health were stretched thin, hanging on the edge. And through it all I kept serving, kept showing up, kept smiling.
No one really saw what it cost me to keep going. I was drowning but in silence.

There came a point when I began to feel it deep within me.
It was not pressure from her but..
A quiet ache. A restlessness. A whisper that grew louder each day "What about me?"
My voice, my needs, my aspirations had faded into the background. I wasn't even aware of how much I had shelved my own self to continue being who I thought I was supposed to be in her presence.
And that pain slowly turned into exhaustion.
That exhaustion turned into quiet resistance.
And slowly, what started as resistance began to feel like a soul's quiet call for space… I needed room to breathe, to be, to exist.
And that quiet unease, over time, became something softer… a tender ache for freedom and ease.

When Anger Became My Wake-Up Call
One day, I could feel my body holding in emotions that had nowhere to go.
The frustration wasn't aimed at her.
It was aimed at my own silence, for how long I had overridden myself to be accepted, to be loved, to belong.

That's when the anger surfaced not to destroy, only to awaken.
It showed me how much of my inner fire I had been suppressing just to keep peace outside.
Without realising that I had reached a point where my constant availability to others no longer felt like kindness but felt like self-neglect.

I knew then, I couldn't keep doing this. My health was at stake. Stress and pressure in my life had crossed boundaries. I was aware no one in their right mind would understand my inner struggle so I had to take a charge.
But I didn't want to hurt anyone.
Especially not the one who had supported me like a mother.
So I didn't say no out loud.
I said it inwardly to the Divine herself. Maa Durga..
Whispered Prayers to the Divine Mother
During the Navratri prayers, I began to speak quietly, just to Maa Durga.
"Please Maa," I would say,
"I can't carry this anymore. Not like this."
It wasn't a rebellion.
It was to surrender to my truth.
I wasn't asking to leave my spiritual mother, I could never.
I was asking to come back to myself.

And then, something I never expected happened.
A couple of years later, my spiritual mother announced that she would no longer continue the Durga Puja celebrations, the very heart of her presence in the community.
It was because of her duties to her mother.
Everyone was stunned.
But I wasn't.
Inside, I was amazed, I knew.. the Divine Mother, Maa Durga heard me.

Even after the festivals stopped, the inner shift took time.
I still felt responsible. I still felt guilty. I still felt the pull of old patterns.
But I began speaking more openly with the Divine, with myself.

I wasn't asking for release out of bitterness.
I was asking for it out of need, a soul need.
To grow.
To breathe.
To find my own rhythm.
To walk a spiritual path that allowed me to expand, not just survive.

Because I had dreams too.. of healing others, of exploring deeper paths, of meeting souls on their journeys.
And somewhere along the way, I began to feel… restricted. Confined.
Like I couldn't move forward while staying where I was.

When Life Moved Me..
There came a point when life pushed me into a corner so tight, I had no option but to break through.
On the home front, things were collapsing emotionally, financially, energetically. We were navigating deep uncertainty, and difficult decisions had to be made, fast.
There was no time to plan, no room to think it through. We had to act. And in that whirlwind, we made a life-altering move… to leave the city.

Everything happened so suddenly, so unexpectedly.
Our life flipped in a matter of days.
We packed up not just our belongings but a lifetime of memories, attachments, routines.
We left behind our home, friends, work, family, everything that felt familiar.

And for me… I left behind my spiritual mother too. That was not easy. But it was necessary.
This wasn't just relocation.
This was divine disruption.
When the Body Speaks, Life Listens
In the middle of all this chaos, my son met with an accident.
A broken ankle..A broken routine..A broken normal.

I didn't think twice.
I left everything and moved cities, this time to Mumbai so I could be by his side during recovery.
And maybe, just maybe, this was life giving me what I had secretly been praying for all along
A pause.. A reset.. A breath..

I didn't realise it then but the Divine had been listening to my pleas..
those whispered longings in the middle of silent nights

"I'm tired.. I want to breathe.. I want to heal.. I want ease.."

A Calling Disguised as Chaos..
What felt like chaos was actually calling.
Calling me out of my comfort zone.
Calling me to release old attachments, old versions of me, old spiritual identities that had run their course.
It wasn't rejection..It was a redirect..

I had always longed to serve, to heal, to hold space for others. But this time, I wasn't doing it by pleasing. I was doing it from alignment. From the truth. From freedom.
This journey moved me away from the city I loved, the people I cared for, even the spiritual foundation I had stood on for decades.

But it moved me toward myself.
And that's where healing truly began.

To this day and till I exist, I'll carry deep respect, reverence and gratitude for my spiritual mother.
She played a monumental role in my life.
I am.. who I am.. because of what I experienced in her presence, both the grace and the gravity.

This chapter isn't about her..It's about me.
It's about a soul that quietly broke free from invisible shackles.. not to run, not to reject but to finally grow.
Because sometimes, love doesn't mean staying.
Sometimes, it means honouring the past, while stepping fully into your own becoming.

The True Power.. the Real power isn't loud.
It doesn't always come through rebellion.
Sometimes, it rises slowly in whispers, in prayers, in the courage to choose yourself without guilt.

I didn't reclaim my power by confronting it.
I reclaimed it by turning inward.

By remembering that the Divine doesn't need a mediator.
It's already within me.

That's the power I live with now.
That's the freedom I was always meant to find.
There was a time in my life when I didn't even realise how much of myself I had handed over…
Not just to a system, not just to society to my family, my parents, to friends, relatives and largely to my spiritual mother.
For years I was chosen by Ma Durga for seva and I honoured her verdict unquestioned, unconditional and unwavering.

But beneath the silence of my service, a storm was brewing.
The truth is I was never allowed to be fully myself around her.
Emotions were to be contained. Feelings weren't to be shown.
And my voice.?

My voice had no place. It was all about..
Endurance.. Obedience.. Survival..
All I wanted was to stay under her shelter… to be accepted, protected, included.
And so I bent.
I even tolerated the unnecessary politics, the hierarchy, the games inside my spiritual group.
Even when it hurt. Even when I felt completely erased.
I kept showing up.
Even when I wanted to scream.. I smiled.
Even when I felt crushed.. I bowed.
Even when I burned inside.. I said nothing.
I said Nothing out of respect, to not hurt my Spiritual Mother or anyone,
And that… was the beginning of my self-abandonment.

Anger became sacred..
Then one fine day.. after one and a half decade of seva, I couldn't take it anymore.

The pent-up anger..The buried frustrations..The silent stress.
The endless expectations coming at me from everywhere, from everyone.

Even from spaces that were meant to feel safe.

People in my spiritual circle..my so-called soul sisters, began questioning my existence.
Casually, almost politely, they brought up fragments of my past, old wounds I had already survived.
Sometimes they wanted answers from my bitter experiences.. Sometimes they wanted relief from their own past.

Either way, I was forced to relive everything again & again..
But this time, the impact came multiplied.

What I had already healed once was being reopened without consent.

Slowly, relentlessly, it began to take a toll.
On my body..On my mind..On my spirit.

The weight became unbearable.
I couldn't hold it for another minute.

For far too long, I had swallowed my emotions.
For far too long, I had kept peace on the outside while waging silent wars within.

But now, those wars refused to stay buried.

They rose..
Raw.. Unapologetic.. Forceful..
And all I could do was watch, like a stunned spectator, as my own inner storm took over.

Even then, I tried to maintain dignity.
I tried not to lash out.
I tried not to confront, blame, or shame.
I tried not to hurt anyone else because I knew exactly what hurt felt like.

But one truth finally anchored itself inside me..

I would not hurt myself anymore.

That day, I made a quiet, unshakable commitment.

I will not abandon my own heart..I will change..I will heal.

And I will trust the path of healing whatever it takes.

The anger I had been suppressing didn't merely rise..

It erupted.

And for the first time, I didn't call it weakness.

I didn't call it failure.

I recognised it for what it truly was.

A boundary.. A signal.. A sacred force asking to be honoured.
And I will trust the path of healing whatever it takes.

The anger I had been suppressing didn't just rise, it erupted.

Not as rage to destroy but as a signal a sacred alarm from my soul saying..
'You are not meant to live like this..'

It was the first time I saw my anger as power.
It wasn't wrong.. It wasn't shameful.. It was truth pure, fiery truth.
A truth I had buried for too long.
I wanted to scream NO. But I didn't scream it to people.
Instead, I turned to the only one who'd listen without silencing me..Maa Durga..!

My Showdown

When the Divine Becomes the Witness.. life unfolds drastically..

In my quietest moments during the Navratri pujas,
I started whispering to Divine Mother, Maa Durga, gently at first, then with desperation
'Please Maa, free me from this seva. I can't do this anymore..'

I still showed up.. Still lit the lamps.. Still decorated the altar.. Cooked all that was advised..
Basically, All the Seva possible..
But inside, I was falling apart. Every act of devotion felt like another chain I was wearing. I wasn't serving from love anymore, I was serving from fear, guilt and duty.

And I kept praying,
'Don't betray me. But I can't betray myself anymore either..'

That was my real showdown with power.
Not a scream. Not a fight.
Just a sacred 'NO' whispered to the Divine.
And the Divine listened..

A year later, without any warning, my spiritual mother suddenly announced that the Durga Puja celebrations, her life's identity, will be conclude for public and only a handful of will be allowed for Seva,
It shocked everyone.
But deep inside, I wasn't shocked. In Awe !
I knew..Maa Durga had heard me..

This wasn't just the end of a tradition, it was the end of a karmic contract. One I hadn't known how to walk away from… so the Divine dissolved it for me.
But the story didn't end there.

Because even after the celebrations stopped, the weight didn't lift immediately. There were still layers of pressure, control and emotional burden I carried. And again, I turned inward not toward people, not toward my spiritual mother but directly to the Divine..
And this was the collapse That set me Free !

Once I started conversations with Maa Durga, like she was my mother & I was confined to Shiva, my guide, my friend, my everything..
After Shiv & Shakti, the mediation dissolved.

And with every word I whispered, I felt lighter.
With every boundary I expressed to them, I felt stronger.
And with every "I can't do this anymore" I said in prayer, the situation outside began to shift.
Slowly, the pressures eased.
The burdens lifted.

The expectations fell away.
And finally, I said:
'I'm done. I don't want to be around people who can't see me..
I want a new life..'

No one can ever take the sacred place that my Guru Maa holds in my heart. My gratitude toward my spiritual mother runs far deeper than words. She did not initiate me into spirituality through convention or comfort but through a way that was entirely her own, demanding yet deeply maternal.
In many ways, she became more than a Guru..she became a mother in the most human sense, holding me, protecting me and tending to emotional needs I did not even know how to name.

There came a phase when her attention toward me grew quieter yet more focused, especially after her Navratris became silent.
It is important for me to say this clearly.. her Navratris did not end because of politics or backbiting.. That noise existed, yes, but it was not the reason.
What unfolded felt far more intentional, far more sacred. I experience it as the play of Maa Durga itself…grace rearranging outer structures so that my Guruma could step away from ritual performance and turn inward toward direct nurturing.

What followed..her discipline, her control, her uncompromising love, was never about punishment or power.
In short a progress towards lightening of my Karmic burden.
It was about opening something within me that had been shut for a very long time.
Something buried deep. Something suppressed. And only a love that was both fierce and maternal could have reached it..Just like Devi Kali !
My Guruma was a tool of Maa Kali to push me away from my comforts only to nudge me into the right direction..

As I was manifesting a life guided by the divine force itself.

A life where I don't serve from fear or guilt. Where I don't seek love through sacrifice.
Where I don't give up on myself to feel worthy.
And I was granted !

My true power didn't come back in a flash.
It returned in whispers..In tears..In prayers.
In the courage to say no not to hurt but to heal.
And now I know power isn't control…Power is clarity !
It's not about walking out in anger.
It's about walking back into yourself.

I love my spiritual mother..I honour her.. She was a big part of my path.

But that chapter is incomplete with this discovery..
'I'm no longer a disciple bound in silence..'
I'm a soul in communion with the Divine directly.
No mediator. No approval needed.
Just me, Maa Shakti and My Shiv…

That is the power I reclaimed.
That is the freedom I now live..

G³ Goonj ~

Here.. Fear was Not the Villain. Silence was..!
There was a time I fought fear like it was the enemy.
I tried to exile it, bury it, outrun it but fear wasn't the monster..
Fear was the wound.
Fear.. was the girl inside me that had been told to hush when all she wanted was to scream.
But the more I resisted, the louder she screamed.
The more I silenced her, the more she grew in the dark.
Until one day, I did something radical.
I sat with her.. And I said,

"I see you. I hear you. But I will lead."
And something miraculous happened. She softened.

Fear wasn't just the monster, it was also the messenger, both !
Fear didn't want control, it just wanted to be acknowledged.
It just wanted to be held.. And when I held it, it stopped roaring.
You see, fear is not what unraveled me..It was the silence around it.

The pretending.. The pleasing.. The performing..
Smiling through those soul-fires I didn't know how to name.
The "I'm fine's" when I was anything but fine.
The way I said "I'm okay" when I was gasping underwater with no hands reaching. That silence..that was the villain..!!

My power was never about slaying fear.
So I stopped trying to slay it..I stopped trying to be fearless.
It was about listening to it.
Letting it speak without letting it steer.

To recognise it… to stay aware… to just stay.. that is power.

Power..!
Power, I've come to learn, isn't the absence of fear.
It's the presence of self, even when fear trembles beside you.
Not the kind that dominates.. The kind that liberates.

So now, I don't conquer fear.
Now, I walk with it.
She trembles beside me.
And I don't push her away.

Because I don't need her gone to be strong.
I just need to keep moving with her.
That is power..!
Not the absence of fear but the presence of self,

I walk beside her with my voice steady, my boundaries clear and my soul leading the way.
That is power..That is freedom..!
That is me.. unraveled, unmasked and finally, whole..!!!

And now I'm aware ..
I can heal.. I am healing.. Not in leaps.. Not in fireworks.
But in sacred, stubborn, small acts.

Choosing to feel instead of numb.. Choosing to stay instead of run.
Choosing me, even when the world forgets to.

Sometimes, the biggest shift happens in the quietest decision.
And sometimes, the greatest revolution…is the day you stop waiting to be saved and come home to yourself instead.
And this?
This was my homecoming.. This was My Beginning !

Best way to express…
It's like walking into a room without the need to convince anyone of anything. It's that quiet confidence that comes from not abandoning yourself for approval, applause or perfectly aligned aesthetics.

And In Your Life?
- Saying no to someone, without guilt when your heart says it's not right.
- Leaving a place, relationship or belief that dishonours your soul even if everyone tells you to stay.
- Speaking your truth softly, yet firmly and not shrinking when no one claps.
- You stop living a double life.. one for the world, one for yourself.
- You finally listen to your inner voice… instead of silencing her with masked productivity or people-pleasing.

- You reclaim the kind of authority that doesn't need followers to feel valid.
- And, most importantly, you make peace with fear without letting her steal the mic.

So in essence.. Holy defiance is…
- Peaceful strength.
- Rooted truth.
- Boundaries without bitterness.
- The kind of rebellion that liberates you.

It's when you choose you.. not out of anger but out of reverence.
It's not a scream.
It's a still, sacred "I'm not abandoning myself anymore."

Fear didn't unravel me.. Silence did !
That is power.. That is freedom.!
You don't have to kill fear. You don't have to be loud. You just have to be real.
And that, my friend, is what we call divine rebellion.
So yes, this piece might not make you levitate by sunrise.
But it might help you stop performing power and start living it.
Now go forth and say 'no' like your soul depends on it..
because, well, it kinda does.
This is not the End. This is the Return..

CHAPTER 26

SHOWDOWN WITH SPIRITUALITY

~SPIRITUALITY WAS SEEKING ME

Spirituality did not enter my life through crisis.
It entered through devotion.

Only later did I understand that it had been seeking me long before awareness arrived.

And somehow… I kept meeting it alone.

Not lonely…Alone..!

Like the soul was being escorted… privately…into its own initiation.

My grooming happened through seva before I even had words for surrender.
Washing utensils… cleaning floors… offering jal… offering food… serving langar…
My parents did something very rare without announcing it… they trained my hands to serve…before my mind learned how to judge.

I was never deeply inclined towards ritual… not the show of it… not the performance of it.
I leaned towards the quiet part… the spiritual part…as if my soul already knew where the real doorway was.

I was born in Gorakhpur, Uttar Pradesh… in the 70s…and my life did not arrive softly. It arrived with cleansing… fast… fierce… almost surgical.

People talk about one rebirth in one lifetime.
I've died many times in this one birth…and survived many times too.
My rebirths didn't wait for "later"… they kept happening while I was still learning how to be a child.

Because when Shiv decides to carve a soul…
it isn't gentle training…it is direct attention.

And the truth is… human senses are not designed to hold God's full frequency.
If He spoke plainly… it would burst our eardrums.
If He showed Himself… the light would blind.
If He touched fully… the body would shatter.

So He doesn't come like a visitor.
He comes like pressure… like purification… like being broke open… again and again…until what is false can no longer survive in you.

Even before I ''understood" anything, the encounters began.
A fever so high the thermometer couldn't register it…my tiny body placed on an ice slab… unconscious… alone…until life returned back into me.

Then a mango orchard…
a sharp stone falling… lodging into my head… breaking the skull open…
blood everywhere… kids running for help…
and me… again… alone… on the ground… with the sky watching.

I didn't know it then…

but this "alone" was not abandonment.
It was a pattern..A signature.

Because the first time I remember spirituality penetrating me…
not as teaching… not as concept…
but as direct experience…like in a temple sermon…

It was in **Harmandir Sahib, Amritsar,**
when I was barely five.

My mother sat upstairs reading her Gutkha… steady… absorbed.
And I sat near the jharokha… watching Guru Granth Sahib being read…
watching people enter and exit like waves…all coming for a glimpse… a blessing… a breath.

My mother went down to bow…
and I… as children do… hopped away.
I wandered around the Sarovar… sprinkling water on myself… playing… smiling, so content… so self-contained… like I didn't belong to anyone but joy.

And then… this thin man…shoulder length uneven hair… shirtless… dhoti… a loose cloth draped… face faint in memory… but the pull… unforgettable.

He gestured… and I followed…
because something in me trusted him without explanation.

He took me to the utensil-washing seva.
Ash mixed with mud… hands moving in rhythm…
rub… rinse… stack…
rub… rinse… stack…

And I joined.

Not as a child trying to copy adults…

as if I was remembering a life I already lived.

Few hours passed…and above me… my mother's world collapsed.

She returned… and I wasn't there.
Panic rose like a storm.
The first fear that came to her was the worst one…she fell into the Sarovar… she's gone…

People searched… staff searched… sevadars ran…
a small child doesn't disappear like that… not inside Harmandir Sahib…
and yet I had.

And when the search had started breaking their hope…
when evening was beginning to settle…
someone saw me.

A tiny girl… alone…washing utensils with ash…
diligent… absorbed…
like the world didn't exist…
like my soul had finally found its language.

That was not "service"…
That was my first initiation.

Because in Gurudwaras… I learned something I still carry.

Holiness is practical.. and service dissolves the self faster than prayer ever can.

Later in life… devotion deepened.

Mystical Navratri's.. taught my body how to wake before desire…
Lamps lit with steadier hands than my thoughts…
Fasting that felt less like sacrifice and more like intimacy…
Mantras that didn't excite the mind… but softened the nervous system.

God arrived as rhythm.
As something dependable..Repeatable..Safe.

And..Seva shaped me before philosophy ever did.
Floors cleaned without ownership.
Langar served without identity.
Hours spent where usefulness mattered more than importance.

Pilgrimage followed naturally.
Kailash did not announce itself… It summoned.
Kedarnath did not reassure… It stripped.
Kashi did not comfort… It confronted.

In Kashi… walking those lanes again and again with my Guru-ma…
I felt watched by something ancient.
Not impressed..Not disappointed..Simply aware.

This is how spirituality blessed my life.
This is how I met God.

Through cut throat discipline…
Through bone deep surrender…
Through devotion that did not negotiate…
And something irreversible unfolded.

For a long time the relationship responded.
I prayed and felt guided… I asked and I felt held.
I trusted and felt answered.

Until one day it stopped..!

No warning arrived.
No mistake announced itself.
God simply went silent.

Not in punishment… Not in withdrawal… In stillness.

At first I assumed it was temporary…

maybe a phase... maybe a test.

I prayed harder.. Longer..With more precision.
I increased my sadhana..Reviewed my rituals.
Checked myself for spiritual negligence.
I gave up what was dear to me... sugar... discarded completely...
Nothing changed..

And the silence stayed.

My Showdown

But my second initiation... the one I can still feel in my skin...
happened even earlier... when I was nine...
At Delhi for a cousin's wedding...
when relatives decided to gather in Rishikesh...and the journey began...

Pilgrimage to Hemkund Sahib Gurudwara & Badrinath...

I remember Badrinath... rice tied in cloth... dipped into the hot spring...
the thrill of cooking prasad in God's own heat...
and right beside it... the ice-cold Alaknanda...
Fire and ice existing together like a scripture.

Then Govind Ghat...overnight at Gurudwara...
and the next day the trek began.

Because I was the only child in the group... my parents hired a **pithu**,
a porter who carries pilgrims in a basket seat... where roads end and faith has to walk.

My mother gave me **Chaupai Sahib** in Hindi...
a prayer like a shield...
and I sat in the basket with the book tucked close like a lifeline.
We rested at Gurudwara Govind Dham.

The next morning… the final trek to Hemkund Sahib began.

At first the pithu stayed with the group.
Then he slowly drifted… chatting… meeting other porters… and without noticing… he took the shortcut route… steep… tough… faster.
10 to 12 porters, and 2 horses, carrying heavy luggage for our group
And I… I was reading.

I had never read Chaupai Sahib before…
I was struggling with the words… forming them… trying…
so engrossed… that I didn't realize the entire world had changed direction.

When I looked up… the terrain was unreal.
Clouds descended so low I could touch them.
The light dipped like evening even though it was morning.
Mist thickened… air sharpened.

Then the pithu put my basket down…
and he and the others disappeared for ten… fifteen minutes…to freshen up.

And there I was again.. Alone..!

And then… snow fall began.
Tiny flakes… delicate… silent…
landing on my cheek like blessings I didn't have vocabulary for.

I stood up and started spinning…
like a doll in a music box…this was all so new.
Chaupai Sahib in one hand… snowfall on my face…
as if the mountain was baptising me… privately.

An old man passed by.
He asked, "Beta… are you alone…?"
Then his eyes fell on the Gutka.

"What are you reading…?"

I showed him the book.
He asked me to read.
So I did… slowly… forming words…

Taa Kaa Moorha Auchaarata Bhedaa…
Jaa Ko Bheva Na Paavata Bedaa…

…and that line that still rings inside me…

Mahaadev ko kehat sadaa siv…
nirankaar kaa cheenat nehe bhiv…

He looked at me and said… "Read this every day."
He touched my forehead…
and left without turning back.

And I don't remember when I dozed off…
only that I woke up to violent movement, the basket back on the pithu's shoulders…
he's running… hopping… cutting through the terrain.

The sun emerged from the clouds and suddenly… heaven opened.

Pink flowers lining both sides of the path…
mist moving like breath…
wind swaying petals like a silent hymn…
and my nine-year-old body… forgetting hunger… forgetting cold… forgetting fear…
because beauty had taken over the nervous system.

The valley of Flowers, showed me a lotus like pink flower… brighter… tougher…
a hard stem… a big bloom…
Brahma Kamalam…
as if nature itself was telling me remember this..you will meet it again.

Later... another halt... local children approached and I joined them... laughter...
then the pithu shouting..
"aachee aachee chito chito"
and I ran back without even knowing the words...
as if my body already understood "come back" is also a divine command.

Hours passed... snow, I collected in my gloved hands became my water... my food...until we reached a tea shop.

And that's where the worlds collided.

My parents... frantic... searching everywhere...
asking porters... scanning faces...
my mother already seeing me fallen into the lake in her mind
that mother-vision that arrives before the news.

And then someone said...a child is sitting near the tea shop.

They came running...and my mother held me like she was holding her
own breath returning.
She cried... thanked God...and I... exhausted... hungry...
dozed off in my father's lap.

At Hemkund Sahib... we had blankets... kangri with burning charcoal...
clouds swallowing vision...among oxygen level dropping... and weather brutal.

And still...

I wandered outside while others hid inside.
I walked to a tiny temple nearby... sat quietly...
as if I belonged more to the cold than to comfort.

Even the bath in the holy pond happened...
a dip that felt impossible in that freezing air...
and my brother's legs freezing in the water... men pulling him out...
boiling water poured to bring life back.

Aaaah..!

That entire pilgrimage...was not just a trip.

It was my soul's first direct training in spiritual reality.

That devotion is not cute.
It is terrain.
It is weather.
It is being lost.
It is being found.
It is being alone with God where no one can interpret it for you.

And that is why... years later...
when God went silent... it didn't begin there.

The silence was only the next grade.

Because the real showdown wasn't when God stopped speaking...

It was when I realised, I did not know who I was without response.

I didn't know me... without reassurance...without signs... without feedback.

Everything I had built my faith on, began to wobble.

I saw it then..

I had learned spirituality through structure.
Through rules... through right methods.

But beneath it all... my relationship with the Divine had turned transactional.

I behaved well to feel shielded.
I stayed devoted to feel chosen.
I practiced spirituality to feel secure.

I was acting out faith… rather than living it.

My goodness was nothing but insurance.
My devotion was nothing but negotiation.
My spirituality was nothing but a safety net.

What I called belief… was performance.

The chants no longer carried me because I was hiding inside them.
The rituals no longer worked because I was using them as armour.
The mantras fell flat because they were recited from habit… not honesty.

This was not abandonment…
This was exposure.

And silence forced me inward.. Not into despair… into truth.

I could no longer borrow certainty.
I could no longer outsource authority.
I could no longer lean on a spiritual identity.

The showdown was brutal.

The God I knew began to dissolve.
the God who rewarded effort..
the God who spoke through signs…
the God who reassured obedience…

That God had to die.

Not because God failed…
but because I had outgrown the version I was clinging to.

True awakening does not arrive as light.
It arrives as loss.

Loss of language...Loss of certainty...Loss of spiritual comfort.

I lost my place in the hymn book...only to gain my own voice.

The Universe does not respond to obedience, It responds to alignment.

And alignment is not about what you do.
It is about who you are when nothing is watching.

The silence was not empty... it was instructional.
It spoke through delays... through doors that did not open... through relationships that fell away... through stillness I tried to escape.

Every unanswered prayer carried truth.
Every pause demanded honesty.
And I had to slow down enough to hear it.

When rituals stop working... you are not being punished.

You are being summoned.

Summoned into a deeper self.
Summoned into way deeper truth.
Summoned into a spirituality that cannot be taught... only remembered.

The fire burned everything that was borrowed.
Everything that was performative.
Everything that was spiritual but not embodied.

What remained was simple.

Shiva was not asking for ritual anymore...
He was asking for surrender.

This was His way… a doorway…and I stepped through it… shaken yet grateful.

Because it was His language…and my body understood before my mind did.

After a few visits to Kashi Vishwanath…
outside the temple… I kept chanting, Om Namah Shivaye, until even the chant disappeared
no voice left to chant… only being.

Breath… Presence… a quiet knowing.

God did not disappear…God moved closer…

Closer than language… closer than belief… closer than form.
Not a voice above me… only a pulse within me.

G^3 Goonj

Spirituality stopped being about ascent. It became about integration.

Not climbing to God anymore…but standing honest in my own breath.

My doubt became prayer…
my rage became sacred…
my silence became communion.

And that is when I understood…

The final stage of spiritual maturity is not saying… "I found God."

It is realising…
I found myself… and God was already there.

Spiritual silence is not absence…

It is the moment the Divine withdraws language… so truth can surface.

If your prayers feel unanswered…
check whether you are speaking from memory… or presence.

If rituals stop working…
ask what they have been protecting you from feeling.

God does not leave…God removes the noise.

And what remains is not belief…
Just alignment.
And alignment does not need reassurance..!

CHAPTER 27

SHOWDOWN WITH THE DIVINE DEADLINE

~WHEN SHIVA CALLS, THERE ARE NO FORMALITIES

Reflects the urgency, the ticking clock around approvals, and how grace doesn't need permission it just opens doors.

It's deeply emotional, poetic, and picturesque retelling my sacred Kedarnath calling…a story that captures the divine orchestration, inner stirrings, and mystical unfolding of this trip as something beyond logic… something only the soul can truly understand

After Kailash Yatra , I had silently vowed No more visits to temples
Not out of weariness, but reverence.
As if Kailash had etched the final punctuation on a sentence long written across lifetimes.
And after Kedarnath, I thought, that will be it..
The last bow. The final visit.
Then I would let the sacred reside fully within me.

But the Divine never follows our plans. It follows the longing buried in our bones.

One evening, I was at a friend's home, dinner flowing into laughter.
Another friend casually mentioned,
"She's going to Kedarnath after a wedding."
And just like that, something inside me cracked open.

It wasn't envy. It wasn't FOMO. But a pull.

Sudden.. Primal.. Fierce..
The kind of pull only a mountain like Kedarnath can have on your soul.

That night, everything changed.
My soul was aware..it was my calling

I asked my friend about the trip. She said it was all arranged by her husband..
"Strict rules, sensitive terrain, special permissions.
You can't just decide and go," she said. There so much planning.. we've planned this months in advance..

Still, my heart wasn't listening to reason. It was already halfway to the Himalayas.

I didn't care who was where.
I walked straight into the room where the men sat, drinks in hand, lost in their own conversations.
I was skeptical
I wasn't that close to my friend's husband..
With a deep breath something moved my legs and I walked towards him..

I interrupted. Politely yet Firmly.
"I need to come with you to Kedarnath. Please… just take me."

He looked at me, surprised.

"It's not that simple Gunj…
The approvals take a couple of weeks.. it's all done and We leave in just a few days. It's barely possible."

And I said what my soul already knew
"Then don't tell me it's not possible. Just try. You've already done the formalities… let me come under your umbrella."

He paused, perhaps caught between doubt and divine timing. Then he said, "Fine. I'll send you the link. Fill it out. If your approval comes through, you're in."

That night I couldn't sleep.
I was restless. Excited. Uneasy…like the soul pacing inside the body.
At 4 a.m., the email with link landed in my inbox.
I opened it instantly, breath shallow, heart racing.

I filled out the form like I was casting a prayer… chanting my mantras as I was breathing through them
Uploaded every document, every ID, every photograph.
And all through it, I kept chanting..
Om Tryambakam Yajamahe Sugandhim Pushti Vardhanam Urvaru Kamiva Bandhana Mrityuh Moskshi Ma Aamritaat…
(Mahamrityunjaya Mantra)

as if my fingers typing were part of a sacred ritual.

At exactly 5 a.m., I hit submit.
Then I whispered,
If this is real, if this is meant to be, if the mountain is truly calling…then make a path, Shiva.

And just like that… I let it go.
No expectations. No hope. Just silence.

Hours passed. I forgot all about it.
Until 3 p.m. that day, when I casually checked my inbox.

There it was..!
The approval.
The very same approval others had been chasing for weeks.

I called my friend's husband in disbelief.
"Check your WhatsApp. I got the approval."
He said, "No way. That's fast..?!?

We've been trying for so long, maybe you got it for next year."

I sent him the screenshot.
He read it. Re-read it.
And finally said, "This is real. This is actually real..!!
Most people get rejected..But lucky you.
Your place was waiting for you.
This trip was destined. Pack your bags.

Application was accepted..
beyond reason…beyond effort…
because the mountain had said Yes.
My Shiva had said yes !

Because when Kedarnath calls, it's not your application that gets approved
It's your soul.

So let me tell you..
this chapter isn't just about a trek to Kedarnath.
This wasn't a tourist trail or just another pilgrimage.
Not just a climb towards the greatest, but a descent…into the deepest layers of soul, karma, and quiet destiny.

It was something far deeper… far older.

It was emotional..It was spiritual.
It was karmic.
A soul-story unfolding in real time.

Each step I took carried layers of memory, longing, surrender.
Every mile held an emotion I hadn't fully felt.
Every bend in the mountain whispered something I once tried to forget.

Mind you, this wasn't just about reaching a shrine.
This was about returning to something I had promised long ago.

So when the mountain called, I didn't ask questions.
I didn't weigh logic.
I didn't check schedules.

I just moved..
because the echo didn't come from outside... it came from within.
The echo of my soul..!
When the calling comes,
You don't plan.
You don't prepare..
You surrender...
You move....!

The divine had already woven the path, crafted each detail with grace too precise for coincidence.
Between fate, faith and fire... something sacred was being set into motion.

All I had to do was say yes.

And just walk.

Because some journeys don't begin when your feet hits the path.. they begin when your soul remembers its contract is coming full circle.

When Strangers Become Fellow Seekers..
And so, I landed in Dehradun.
The air carried that quiet Himalayan chill gentle but undeniable..
the kind that brushes against your skin like a whisper from something greater.

My friends were already in Rishikesh, busy with wedding rituals, but my path was about to take its own shape.

Just as I stepped out with my luggage, my phone rang.
It was her my friend from our group.

"Another friend just landed too..from the U.S.," she said.
"You don't know her, but you'll know her soon enough. She's family now.
Find her, wait for her.. Hire a car…Start your drive to Rishikesh together."

And so I waited.

A sea of people passed by. Luggage wheels rolled across floors. And then there she was tired-eyed, jet-lagged, a little surprised, glowing with that unmistakable energy of someone who had also been called by something larger than herself.

We greeted each other like old souls meeting after lifetimes..
No awkwardness, no pretences.. just an immediate, quiet recognition.

We started our journey toward Rishikesh, but first took a detour. She insisted we go see the highest point of Dehradun before heading onward.
So we drove up, winding roads weaving through mist and green.

From that elevation, the city looked miniature.
Silent.. Still..
A perfect contrast to the inner movement both of us were beginning to feel.

There, at that height, she began to open up.

Softly at first..
about her fatigue, her doubts, the heaviness she hadn't unpacked.
How even amidst all the achievements and apparent stability of life in the U.S.,
something in her felt unsettled.
Untouched..Unseen..

She said, "I don't even know why I came… but something told me I had to."

And I knew exactly what she meant.
Because I didn't come for the view either..
I came for the purge.

Some journeys begin with flight tickets, others begin with wounds.
And some, like this one began.. the moment two strangers look at each other and silently say
"I see you. I know what brought you here."

We landed into a sea of chaos.. Dehradun bursting at the seams, tourists crawling through jammed roads like slow-moving rivers. What should have been a two-hour drive to Rishikesh took nearly four.

Buzzing Crowds.. Dust.. Noise..
But beneath all that, something was guiding the silence in me.

We finally reached our friend hotel…the one who, with her husband had come for the wedding, who had helped plan everything.
But grace never follows human convenience.
Her husband was already down with a fever.
And by nightfall, she too messaged me… high fever, weak, unsure if she could travel.
The entire trip…this divinely orchestrated dream, suddenly hung by a thread.!

The Chaos..
I lay awake in that hotel bed, restless.
Not just with excitement but with anxiety
Had I come all this way only to turn back now..?
Was I foolish to believe that destiny would part traffic, fever, and fate for me..?

Tears rolled silently onto the pillow.
Not loud grief.. but sacred disappointment.

The kind only seekers feel when the door to God feels like it might be closing again.

But Fate was Pushing Forward..
Anyway in the morning, everything still felt uncertain.
But we went to see them, sick or not.
And what we heard was unexpected !

"You're going," her husband said. "Everything's booked. Everything's arranged.
Hotels, cabs, helicopter. Don't let our absence stop you. Just go."

It wasn't a suggestion.
It was a divine command delivered through a human voice.
I understood…This trip is designed just for the two of us.

And we began are divinely planned journey..
The Roads.. the Rivers.. the Realisations..

Two strangers boarded the cab, two women, barely prepared, filled with more faith than knowledge.. into the oblivion.

As we crossed Devprayag, where the Bhagirathi and Alaknanda rivers merge to become the Ganga,
The confluence was so alive..
I stood in the sharp Himalayan sun, watching that meeting.
Two distinct forces becoming one.
Just like me.. still fragmented, but beginning to merge.

With spirit... With purpose.. With the divine..

The Ticket No One Could Get.. But We Did !
At Guptkashi, we rested briefly, then drove another hour through the freezing dusk to collect our helicopter passes.
What we found was overwhelming hundreds waiting, many for days, some for weeks, due to uncertainty of weather
The air buzzed with frustration.

We held hands.
Two women cutting through a sea of uncertainty and testosterone.
Holding a letter, a thread of belief, and each other.

And then grace again..
The officer approved us.
Just like that.
And all I could think was… if they knew how we got these tickets, there would be chaos.

But when Shiva wants you in His home, He clears paths no one else sees.

That Night of Flying Bugs, Fading Fears and Fierce Bonding Where sleep was again Elusive.

Our room was infested with flying bugs, lizards, crawling creatures that challenged our comfort and our courage.
My friend was terrified and I found myself slaying bugs like some mountain warrior.

It was absurd. It was hilarious. It was divine training.
Because you don't meet gods in sanitised luxury.
You meet them in wild rooms, sleepless nights and laughter laced with madness.

Somewhere between clearing bugs and clearing pain, we spoke deeply.
Of wounds.. Of truths.. Of what brought us here..

And in that rawness, we bonded.
Not as traveler's but as karmic companions.

Then Shiva came with Coffee and Upma..
At 4:30 a.m., we rushed for the helipad.
Frozen fingers. Breath hanging in the air.
People were being flown out based on old waiting lists from yesterdays cancellations due to bad weather

No food. No tea. Just patience.
Patience under that half covers shed..
And then… a miracle in a paper cup.

A fellow seeker from a senior citizen group saw us shivering, offered us coffee and upma by requesting their caterer.
It wasn't just a hot drink it was Shiva's prasad.

I took it in my hand, and I swear I didn't taste coffee.
I tasted kindness.. ..Warmth Divine timing..Immense Love..

An overwhelming reminder:
when the mountain calls you, it feeds you, warms you and carries you even through strangers.

The Flight Into the Heart of the Divine..
A sudden weight mismatch in another group gave us a jump in queue.
My friend sat next to the pilot. I sat alone behind as I wanted it to be.
No chatter.. No curiosity..Just stillness.

As we flew, I didn't want to talk.
I wanted to merge.
With the sky..The rivers.
The Himalayas below..The rising silence within me.

Few minutes flight, with breathtaking, spectacular views of Himalayas from merely a few hundred feet…we landed in Kedarnath.

We hugged each other jumping with joy..
We were only digesting this surge of happiness..
Just then I realised.. valley didn't welcome us with fanfare.
It embraced us with silence.

Cold air.. Crisp smell.. Sacred stillness.

Something in me… stopped.

Very efficiently we were greated by two swami's upon landing, who said they were sent by Shiva Himself.
They guided us through the throng, narrating the legend of the Pandavas and the elusive Shiva who disguised Himself as a bull. And this is the place from where Pandavas left for heaven and we loved the narration while we were in the Que for another half an hour..

Then came the moment.
The Four sides of Shiva..!
The Garbhagraha…the inner sanctum.

"Women not allowed," the guard said.
I requested the swami's pleaded..
But he didn't listen and pushed us away..

Few minutes later I looked him in the eye and whispered,
"Then don't see me as a woman."

He stepped aside..

Inside, a very unusual Shivling stood tall, massive, raw, alive in the form of a bull's hunch or many describe as trikone.(somewhat in a triangle)

I didn't just bow once. I was called to bow on all four sides.
The Sadhu kept asking me to touch my head to the Shivling as if he never saw me do it the last time.
Each side and each time I bent, it wasn't just my body…it was another lifetime .
Each time I touched my forehead, it wasn't just reverence…it was release.

By the fourth side, my body was suspended in mid-air, stretched in ways I didn't know was humanly possible
And somehow, I reached.

Again..
As I touched my head to the fourth side, Something cold entered from the centre of my forehead and gave me chills and shivers down my spine..
My throat dry..My hands numb ..Me frozen !

I felt each and every movement of that energy entering me..
No I was not intimidating just receiving..

My Showdown

While the sadhus were offering prayers for our family's lineage
I was in another Realm.
I was participating in that ritual but zoned out !!
Back into the inner sanctum with that energy vibrating inside me like a tiny fairy bouncing and touching each and very cell of my existence.

The Return That Almost Wasn't..
In minutes the the skies darkened.

Locals whispered, "They won't fly today." "All trips will be cancelled"
The mountains swallowed our optimism.
But I had seen enough by now to know…when Shiva opens the door…
He doesn't shut it midway.

And sure enough, an hour later, the clouds parted.
We were flown back to safety though we faced little turbulence and anxieties came creeping in.. But faith was strong as ever.

The moment our feet touched ground the weather crashed again.

All flights cancelled.

But we had made it.
By seconds.. By blessings. ..By something no logic can name.

G^3 GOONJ ~

Some journeys don't end when you return.
They echo.!
In your cells. In your breath. In the way your heart beats softer when you speak of God.
Kedarnath did not just give me darshan, It dismantled me to reassembled me.
As something quieter, lighter, closer to who I was always meant to be.

I didn't go there to pray for something.
I went there to remember who I am without everything I thought I needed.

I didn't go there to be heard.. I went there to listen
To the silence inside stone..To the stillness inside surrender
To the love that doesn't speak in words, but moves in winds and mountain shadows.

I learned that sometimes, the Divine doesn't call the strongest.
It calls the readiest..
And when it does, your only task is to say yes
Even when you're unprepared.
Even when the path is unclear.
Because grace doesn't ask you to be perfect.
It asks you to be available.. Available to receive..!

I learned that real faith isn't loud.
It's the quiet courage to walk toward something
you can't see, can't prove, but feel…in your bones.

I learned that when the time is right,
not even closed doors, sick friends, or clouded skies can stop your soul from reaching where it's meant to go.

And above all…

I learned that Shiva does not live in temples.
Shiva lives in the part of me…in you.,
that walks when every reason says stop.

That believes when logic says doubt.
That bows when ego says run.

This wasn't just my last temple visit.
This was my first real homecoming.

And for that,
I do not just offer gratitude.
I offer my entire being.

To the planners.. To the navigators
To the mountain..To the calling.
To the grace that guided me through.
To the God that lives, not above but within.

As I stood under the open sky, hands folded, eyes moist
I wasn't just thanking Shiva.

I was thanking life..Thanking grace..Thanking the unseen orchestration that made this impossible journey inevitable.

This was not a trip…This was a soul retrieval.

And as we drove away from Kedarnath, I didn't feel like I was leaving a temple.
I felt like I was carrying it home.

CHAPTER 28

SHOWDOWN WITH SLEEP

~THE NIGHT KAILASH HELD ME

'After years of sleepless nights.. It wasn't a warm bed or quiet room that gave me peace..It was a storm, a prayer and a mountain.'

When Sleep Becomes Sacred
The journey had already been fierce rivers that roared in fury, rains that lashed with no mercy, and trails that tested the body and spirit alike.
We had just arrived at Dirapuk. The air was thin, the winds sharp, clouds in multiple shades and Kailash stood before us like a silent guardian cloaked in snow, crowned in sunlight. I had soaked in every second of that majestic darshan. But as we reached the north face of Kailash, the skies parted. For a fleeting hour, sunlight bathed the peak in gold, and I walked in silent reverence, hypnotised by the play of snow and light.

I had meditated with monks, watched the mountain dance with light, and breathed in the stillness that only such altitudes carry. It was overwhelming in the best way.
But Kailash has its own rhythm. And it shifts without warning.
By the time we finished our early meal, the sun had vanished behind thick clouds, and darkness crept in at 3pm. The air turned electric and the rain in shrapnel.. The Swamiji, a seasoned pilgrim on his 11th trip here, was narrating tales of past yatras, and he had never seen such rains ever..

Then the storm whispered at first, just a drizzle. By the time my group completed the trek from Yamdwar to Dirapuk, that whisper had become a roar. Rain lashed the mountains, and the wind howled through the silence of Tibet. Those who were minutes behind me were caught in a furious downpour that wouldn't stop till morning.

We were staying in metal containers converted into makeshift rooms. And when hail hit tin, it wasn't just noise it was a war drum. Every drop echoed like thunder, rattling our bones. Then came the leak. Right in the middle of the container room. A steady stream of icy water fell onto one of the beds of an elderly woman. She had already endured the wrath of rain on the trail, and now, drenched and trembling, she sat on a soaked bed in subzero cold.

We all tried what we could heating pads, dry clothes, spare blankets. I offered her my dry bed. We emptied the wet mattress and left it untouched, its soaked blankets smelling of cold, damp neglect. Not one bed was in good shape to begin with. The entire room every bed, every blanket was a testament to wear, dampness, and cold neglect.

My Showdown

This was not rest. This was survival. Stains of time and hardship lingered in the fabric, in the air. But it wasn't comfort we had come for.. it was the Darshan, the Divine sighting.

As instructed, that night, there was no lying down. At 17,000+ feet with no acclimatisation, we were warned… sleeping the wrong way, oxygen drops fast. Many collapse that way.

So, we sat. Legs outstretched, backs straight, heads propped with pillows. A strange posture for rest, yet the only option.

And then it happened..

As I leaned slightly back and let my body fall into stillness, I felt something unexplainable. Glimpses of the day flashed before me..

The hotel in Tibet, bus ride, the walk to Yamdwar, ohh..the divine sunlight on the north face of Kailash, sipping salty tea, the unusual rainfalls, crossing live streams.. Those images took over my senses and I was completely soaked into its essence as It played like a silent film, alive in front of me.
Alongside. feeling of wetness all around.. the smell of soaked wet thick cotton blankets..sound of hail and rain landing on our tin roof.. mixed with body odour of 8 women in the tin container, who haven't showered in days.

The body surrendered into everything at once the
dampness in the air, the heavy scent of rain-soaked cotton blankets, the quiet closeness of many bodies sharing a small space. Rain and hail found the tin roof and stayed there, rhythmically, patiently, persistently.. like a lullaby that didn't ask for attention. The body stopped resisting the night. And without realising when or how, I slipped into a sleep so deep it felt less like rest and more like being held.

Hard to believe but the deepest sleep I had ever known.
Not the kind that comes with silence or comfort. Not the kind wrapped in warm sheets. But the kind that feels like being held. Like being lowered into the arms of something larger than love something ancient, something holy. I didn't care about my shoes still on, the layers of damp wool, the cold metal floor beneath me. I wasn't even sure I was breathing the way I should at that height. Because I was floating.

It felt like sleeping in the lap of the kindest Mother.. Like being tucked into the folds of a divine robe. Like resting my head on the shoulder of the strongest protector in the universe. I was safe.. I was light.. And I was gone..

For those two hours, I disappeared. Wrapped in layers of clothing, shoes still on, back barely rested ..none of it mattered. I wasn't lying in a leaking container.
I was floating in a timeless space..Cradled..Weightless..Tethered in space..

Two hours hours passed like seconds.
And when I opened my eyes, I wasn't groggy. I was awakened in a way no meditation or mantra had ever made me feel. That sleep didn't just rest my body. It aligned my spirit. It was sacred.
I didn't plan to sleep. I wasn't even allowed to. But something bigger took over. And I surrendered without even knowing I was doing it.

That sleep wasn't ordinary…It was holy..
That sleep was not ordinary.As if Kailash itself held me…As if the mountain said, "Enough. Rest now..!"It felt as though Kailash itself had drawn me close, holding me into the warmest embrace.. without effort or demand.

It felt as though Kailash itself had drawn me close, holding me into the warmest embrace.. without effort or demand.
In that holding, something in my body loosened quietly releasing what it had been carrying for too long.
Nothing dramatic..Nothing forced..
Just a gentle emptying, as if the mountain absorbed all the unnecessary negativity hovering over me from ages.

I slept like a child in the lap of God…. Sometimes, sleep doesn't come when you want it most like all those nights insomnia mocked me. But when it does arrive uninvited, unexpected… it comes as medicine. As mercy. As magic.
That night, Kailash didn't just give me Darshan… It gave me the much needed rest.

When I finally left Kailash, the difference was unmistakable.

It wasn't only the body that felt lighter. A weight had lifted from somewhere far deeper, off my breath, off my spirit, off my soul, off my lives…a part of me that had been tired long before it had words.

Sometimes, the rest we need doesn't come when we chase it. It comes when we surrender.

And when it comes it heals more than the body.

It heals the soul.

G³ GOONJ~

We often chase rest the way we chase peace as if it's something we have to earn, control or schedule. But true rest, like grace, arrives when we stop trying. It flows when we surrender.

At 17,000 feet, in the heavens of Himalayas, that night at Dirapuk, in that harshest cold, amid leaking roofs, wet beds, and howling wind..

I learned something so powerful..

Sleep doesn't always come from comfort.

Sometimes, it comes from being cradled by something far greater.. the Divine itself..!

And in that sacred surrender, I found the kind of restoration that no medicine, no mantra, no night of luxury could give.

So if you've been chasing sleep, chasing stillness… maybe stop chasing.

Maybe the peace you seek is already seeking you.

Let it find you.

Even in a storm…when you least expect it.

There something profound I want to add here..

No one speaks of this part of a pilgrimage.

No one talks about this side of a pilgrimage.

Not the spiritual highs but the raw, gritty mess beneath it.

The part where your body is screaming, your breath is heavy, your head is pounding and you wonder…
why am I doing this..?
Is God not present everywhere..?

They talk about the Darshan…Strange experiences…The Kora…
The peace…The Divine light..
But they don't talk about the pain it takes to get there.
How your legs shake, how you can't sleep, how your fingers freeze even when your heart is burning with devotion.
They don't talk about the nights you lie awake,
doubting if your body will even carry you through the next day.
But still something pulls you.
It's not logic.. and for sure..It's not planning..
It's something deeper. A
Like a soul-magnet.
Because you don't choose this journey. .It chooses you.

And even when everything hurts, even when the path feels brutal and the air feels too thin to breathe, there's this strange quiet inside that says keep going.
Quite that chatter…Connect with that silence..

That's the thing no one tells you..that grit is part of the grace.
The hardship doesn't take you away from the divinity.. it prepares you for it.
It strips you down, so when you finally stand before the sacred…
You don't just see God.
You feel seen by God.
You feel seen by you..

CHAPTER 29

SHOWDOWN WITH KARMA

~THE DEBT COLLECTORS OF KARMIC CURRENCY

Karma is a cosmic accountant.
Neat.. Impartial.. Mathematical.
What You Owe the Universe..

No one never explain is how it actually collects..?

Chitragupt does not arrive in ceremonial robes or a golden crown.
He does not quote scripture.
He does not announce himself or warn you of consequence.

Most of the time it slips in quietly.
As a broken phone.. A leaking ceiling..
A vehicle that refuses to cooperate the moment you are already stretched thin.
A medical bill that appears uninvited and refuses to leave.

You look at the timing and feel wronged.
Why now.. Why this.. Why when I was finally steady..?

And somewhere between irritation and disbelief a deeper discomfort rises.

A part of you already knows.
Not in language..in weight.

Maybe you did ask for this.
Not consciously....Not deliberately.

But through something unfinished.

Let me tell you a story..

There was a man I knew. Let us call him Arjun.

He was generous in bursts and absent when responsibility demanded continuity.
Years ago a friend lent him fifty thousand rupees when he was struggling. Not as charity, as faith.

I will return it in a month he said easily.

The month passed..Then another.
Then life improved and excuses grew subtler.
By the time Arjun had the money his pride had already rewritten the story.

It is been too long now. He will manage. I will settle it someday.

That someday never came. He kept chasing and hiding from his friend..

A year later his bike engine collapsed. Repair cost twenty two thousand.
Two months after that his phone slipped from his hand. Screen shattered. Thirteen thousand gone.
Then a toothache escalated into a root canal, Fifteen thousand more.

Different incidents..Different explanations..

Same total.

Life was not punishing him..It was collecting.

Karma rarely returns in the same form.
It returns in the same value.
It does not track your memory lapses.
It does not negotiate with intention.
It works on integrity.

On energetic balance.
On what was taken and never restored.

You borrowed from someone's trust and left the account open.
Now the universe borrowed from yours.

Not dramatically but Efficiently.
This is not only about money or transaction.
It never is.
It is about emotional debts that feel invisible until they mature.

My Showdown

Karma arrived through endurances I could not have imagined when the story first began.
Losses that did not ask permission.
Delays that tested every remaining thread of patience. Repetitions that felt unnecessary until they were no longer ignorable.
I endured not because I was strong but because there was no exit.

Chitragupt does'nt arrive in robes or golden crown for me either..
My showdown with him was quieter.

It did not come as fear.. It came as recognition.

A moment when I stopped blaming timing, luck, people, systems.
A moment when the pattern stood still long enough for me to see it.

I realised this was not life being unfair.
This was life being precise.

Every delay I had justified.. Every return I had postponed.
Every silence I had chosen over discomfort.
They were not forgotten.. They were waiting.

That was the confrontation.
Not dramatic. Not punishing.

Just the uncomfortable clarity that nothing I had left incomplete had disappeared..It had only changed form.

In that moment I understood something unsettling and liberating at once.

And then one day awareness descended quietly. Not as relief but as perspective.
What once felt like punishment rearranged itself into instruction.
The weight did not vanish but its meaning changed.
I was not being attacked.
I was being asked to take responsibility for my own energetic footprint.

And in that shift something fundamental transformed.
I stopped asking why this was happening to me and began seeing what it was asking of me.

That was my showdown with karma.
Not when something broke.
But when denial did.

Did you walk away from someone who loved you without giving them closure..?
Did you promise presence and vanish when it became inconvenient..?
Did you take someone's time care effort belief and exit as though it was nothing..?

Then do not be surprised when silence starts meeting you halfway.
When support thins.
When opportunities stall for reasons no one can explain.

This is not revenge.
It is education.

Karma does not hurt you to shame you.

It mirrors you so you can finally feel what you once placed in someone else's life.

And yes it can feel harsh.
But karma is not cruel.
It is exact.

If you owe life will collect.
If you give life will return it often sideways often delayed often disguised as luck.

The most dangerous part is not the debt.
It is forgetting that you ever had one.
And the universe never forgets.

So when something keeps breaking, draining, leaking, ask a better question.

Not.. why me
But what did I leave unsettled..?

Sometimes the cracked the TV screen is not clumsiness.
It is a reminder.
You owe.
And the universe has impeccable bookkeeping.

Now all about…Clearing the Ledger

Here's the truth most spiritual conversations skip.
Karma is not interested in revenge.
It is interested in restoration.

It does not want you to suffer.
It wants you to notice.

To feel the weight you once placed in someone else's world.
So you stop carrying it unconsciously in your own.

Awareness is the turning point.

Once you see that what you owe is not only financial but energetic..
your word.. your time.. your presence.. your respect.. perspective changes.

You stop borrowing what you cannot return.
You stop promising what you do not intend to keep.
You stop taking unless you are willing to restore in full in faith in form or in humility.

You begin to live lighter.

You settle an old bill even symbolically.
You send the message you delayed for years.
I never said thank you properly, I owe you that.

You stop justifying what you withheld and start correcting the pattern.
Become someone who does not leave energetic residue behind.
Because freedom is not only about what you earn.

It is about what you no longer owe.

The learning is simple and sacred.
Your karma is your currency.
And the goal is not perfection.
It is integrity.

Not because everything was paid.
But because everything was honoured.

When you arrive at this understanding the shift happens.

The unexplained breakdowns slow down.
The invisible leaks stop.
What remains is clarity, peace and a subtle inner knowing.
With a loud inner humm..
All dues cleared, you may proceed.

Lets go Beyond the Moral Story of Karma..
Most people understand karma as a moral scoreboard.
Good deed-bad deed reward punishment.

That is kindergarten karma.
There is a shadow layer that rarely gets named.

Karma does not always return in identical form.
It returns in substituted impact.
You may not lose what you took.
But you may lose what you loved.

A child who resents you for reasons you cannot trace.
A creative flow that dries up without explanation.
A business that never quite lifts despite multiple efforts.
A persistent sense of being unseen, unsupported stalling.

That relationship that should have worked but slipped through your fingers for no clear reason.

These are not random.
They are echoes.
Karmic frequency does not replicate the act.
It replicates the impact.

Now What Few Are Willing to Admit..
Karma is not only about what you did.
It is also about what you allowed.

You saw something unjust and stayed silent.
You benefited from someone else's loss even passively.
You let another suffer because speaking up would have cost you comfort.

This rarely gets labeled as wrongdoing.
But the soul records it.

And the universe restores alignment not just action.

The real karma is not..you did wrong.. now suffer !

It is.. You stepped out of truth now return

G³ Goonj~

A Golden Tip Sealed in Grace..
Karma Can Be Cleared Without Performance..
This part is almost never spoken.

You do not always repay karma publicly or dramatically.
Some of the deepest clearing happens quietly.

You bless those you hurt without expecting reconciliation.
You give anonymously to someone living the pain you once caused.
You stay back for someone even when it disrupts your plan.

You offer kindness in the direction of your old wounds especially if you once held the blade.

These acts do not announce themselves.
But they shift timelines.
And what Karma responds to is sincerity not spectacle.
Before forgetting let me tell you..
Timing Is Karma's Softest Weapon.
When you delay doing the right thing the cost multiplies.
Not as punishment but as pressure.

Karma whispers first.
When ignored it speaks louder.

Debt compounds only because release was postponed.

You cannot escape karma but you can always convert it into grace by meeting it early and this happens in the Right Divine timing, called Awareness at the right time..!

Let This Truth Speak Aloud…

Karma is not your punishment..it's your permission.
Permission to evolve.
Permission to end patterns that were never yours alone.
Permission to stop passing pain forward.

When you heal a karmic loop you are not just helping yourself. You are clearing ancestral residue and Interrupting inherited wounds.
Ensuring your children do not bleed for debts they never incurred.

That is not spirituality..That is responsibility..!
Imagine karma not as a judge but as a scribe.
Quiet.. Patient.. Writing in a book you never read directly.

Every time you take without gratitude.
Every time you delay a return.
Every time you speak without care.

Ink moves..

And the ledger is not only yours.
It carries names before you and after you.
You're mere part of an unfinished sentence.

Now imagine yourself as a vessel.
You ask for abundance love clarity yet nothing stays.
Because karma creates leaks.

Until truth is faced.. until apologies are made.. until integrity is restored the universe can pour endlessly and you will still feel empty.

Years ago I lent someone a few hundreds.
A small amount.. Almost forgettable.

They promised to return it in two days.
They never did.

I let it go externally.

Internally something stayed open.

Strangely that exact amount kept disappearing from my life.
An overcharged auto.
A broken bottle.
A useless expense.

Five hundred gone again and again.

Until one day I understood..this was not about money.
It was about closure.

I sat quietly and acknowledged it fully.
I forgive you.
I forgive myself for holding silence instead of truth.
Let this be complete.

From that day onward the leak stopped.

That was when it became clear.

I'm sure this chapter gives you a perspective on karma like no other. This is only pure grace what I share.

Remember..
Karma does not always want your money.
It wants your mindfulness..

CHAPTER 30

SHOWDOWN WITH DUALITY

~THE HORSEMAN, THE STORM AND THE HAND THAT HELD ME

A confrontation with divine duality, karmic endurance, and the paradox of grace through suffering.

All through the disruption I asked..
Why did you call me here, Shiva?
Why summon me across borders, breathless terrains, and frozen faith only to be tormented again?

I had dreamt of the horse ride from Yamdwar to Dirapuk as a sacred yatra, a slow ascent into silence. I thought I would merge into your rhythm..the wind, the mantras, the pulse of eternity echoing through the cliffs of Kailash.

But instead, my journey began with chaos. My horseman, a young, restless seventeen-year-old Tibetan boy, carried not devotion but defiance.
With a Bluetooth speaker hanging from the horse's neck, he blared loud Tibetian pop music, that sliced through the stillness I had come seeking. When I pleaded for silence, he smirked, ignored and worse hit my thigh with that very speaker, not once but a few times as and when i requested to switch off the music

Each blow wasn't just physical. It was an assault on my faith, my peace, my prayer. My fellow traveler, my soul-sister and my porter kept asking him to stop, but his eyes were wild, untamed and kept yelling and smoking..Perhaps anger was his only language. Perhaps my silence enraged him more.

And in that moment,
I asked Shiva..
Is this how you welcome your devotee?
Why am I being tested again, when all I seek is You?

But just when despair was beginning to creep through my bones, came Pempa. My porter. Barely four feet tall, gentle eyes and a smile that could melt the mountain cold. He didn't know Hindi or English.. only the chant "Om Namo Shiva" and helped me down the horse and in sign language asked me to walk..

He carried my bag, and unknowingly, pieces of my faith too. Whenever a stream crossed our path, he would leap on the stones, turn back, stretch his hand, and whisper "Shiva…"
All throughout many big and small streams due to non-stop rains and cloud bursts.
Each time, I held his hand and I swear, it wasn't Pempa holding me..
It was grace itself.

He became my silent protector in this storm of contrasts the one who sang hymns while hopping across slippery rocks, the one who reminded me that compassion doesn't need translation.

And so, I started walking more, riding less. I wanted to stay close to this quiet strength, this unnamed guardian who held devotion like breath.
The further we walked, the more the weather tested us..sudden rain, piercing winds, thunder cracking through the valleys. But even amidst it all, the rhythm of Pempa's chant held me anchored.

My Showdown

The mountain mirrored the turmoil inside me. The storm outside felt like the rage within..the outrage at being hit, the helplessness of not being understood, the disillusionment that even sacred journeys could bruise.

Even the tent were filled with people sipping salty tea and yam meat and my heart didn't permit me to enter..

The rain lashed like accusation. The clouds turned black as guilt. The path became slippery with exhaustion. Every part of me wanted to collapse not from pain, but from disbelief.

Yet, through it all, Pempa's hand would appear again, in a thin knit glove torn in many places, steady, grounded, offering faith in motion.
The same world that had humiliated me now offered me healing in another form.
That's when I understood this was no ordinary journey. It was a karmic theatre.

Kailash doesn't call you for comfort.
He calls you for cleansing.
Every bruise, every humiliation, every storm is part of your karmic peeling.
The horseman was my mirror…a reflection of anger I had once carried, the echoes of past lifetimes where I may have misused power or wounded others' faith.
And Pempa… he was my redemption, a living embodiment of service, humility, and grace.

When I finally reached Dirapuk, the storm broke open like an emotional dam. The North Face of Kailash emerged drenched in golden light, its crown glistening through retreating clouds. It felt as though the mountain was breathing again and with each exhale, my resentment dissolved into reverence.

I fell to my knees, tears blending with rain, whispering
"Now I understand, Shiva. You didn't call me here to punish me.
You called me here to purify me."

Transformation kicked in like a Bit b12 shot and I saw things in actual..

I had come broken.
Not curious.. Not seeking answers..
I had come wanting to dissolve. To merge with divinity and not return to the life I was exhausted by.

And instead, I was given the horseman.
Rough.. Loud.. Relentless.
As if the mountain first met me with friction.

Then there was Pempa.
Maybe he was the single narrow ray of light in that chaos.
My Porter, allotted to me by divine lottery.

Hopping across one of the streams, Pempa stumbled.
Nothing dramatic. Just a slip on wet stone.

But what followed stayed with me.

He grew visibly nervous.. Almost embarrassed..
At lunch, he didn't sit close. He hovered at a distance as if he had failed some unspoken responsibility.

That's when it struck me.
My godsent helper has flaws.

Later, when his foot slipped again on stones, he laughed loudly at himself.
No apology. No explanation. Just laughter cutting through the rain.

He carried my bag.. My water bottle.. Step after step..
Of course he got tired.

I saw it in the faint smile he tried to hold in place.

When I caught that smile, we stopped. We ate. We didn't speak but we sand hymns.

For a moment, my emotions placed him on a pedestal.
As if relief itself needed a face.

And then I saw it clearly.
No human could compete with the divine force that had designed both the pain and the comfort of this journey.

Pempa was not grace itself.
He was how grace chose to pass through.

An then the Epiphany at this play of Divinity…
The Divine isn't always kind..
Sometimes, He teaches through contrast, through the sting and the salve, the slap and the solace.
You don't ascend to Kailash untouched.
You arrive raw, stripped, exposed…only to return hollowed and holy.

The horseman tested my endurance. Pempa restored my faith.
And between them, I met the mirror of duality… that all darkness carries the seed of light and every cruelty hides an invitation to compassion.

G³ Goonj ~

Duality is not an accident of life… it is its design.
Every soul walks through the world between two poles…
the kind and the cruel,
the storm and the sunlight,
the silence and the scream.
We often ask why the Divine lets both exist..?
But duality is the language through which consciousness evolves.

The horseman and Pempa were not opposites.. they were parts of one truth. One came to expose my pain… the other came to reveal my power.
One hit my body..the other healed my heart..
One showed me how noise can desecrate devotion… the other showed me how devotion can dissolve noise.

In life too, we meet these two forces every day…people who hurt and people who hold, moments that test and moments that soften, shadows that haunt and lights that heal.

The mistake is not in facing duality, but in forgetting that both exist for our refinement.

When you see both as sacred the pain that pushes and the peace that soothes… you rise above polarity and step into oneness.
How can Shiva allow such cruelty in his own vicinity..?

All the horsemen, porters and shop owners, all who reside in Shiva's vicinity are ganas, his devoted companions,
beyond any social order and spiritual hierarchy, just under his grace and fierce compassion.
That is where Shiva resides not on one side of your experience but at the centre of both.

At Kailash, I didn't just witness the mountain…I witnessed the truth that divinity expresses itself through duality.
And when you bow to both the storm and the sunlight you don't just survive the pilgrimage…
you complete it.

When you are summoned to Kailash, you do not come as a tourist.
You come carrying the weight of your karmic debts… each step, a transaction of grace.
You endure storms not as punishment, but as purification.
The rude horseman was not my enemy.. he was my mirror.

The gentle porter was not my saviour.. he was my reflection of what I am becoming.

Between pain and prayer, between wound and wonder…I met myself..!

And in that meeting, I saw Shiva not as a deity on a peak,
but as the pulse running through every contrast,
whispering…
"I am in both… the one who hurt you, and the one who healed you."

CHAPTER 31

SHOWDOWN WITH THE UNWRITTEN GREY ZONES

~WHEN LIFE DARES YOU TO FIND GOD IN THE FOG

There are places in life that do not come with closure.
No tidy endings.. No clear beginnings..
Just a fog.
A pause..A heartbreak mid-sentence..A purpose still forming.
A question echoing long after the room has emptied.

I have lived there.

The unwritten grey zones.

Those spaces where you do not know whether to hold on or let go.
Whether to fight or surrender.
Whether it is ending or quietly beginning in a language you do not yet understand.

They arrive without warning.
Not as events but as conditions.
A state of being where certainty dissolves and instinct has not yet learned how to speak.

The ache of almost's and maybe's lives here.

I remember standing outside an ICU barefoot bargaining with the sky.
Someone I loved was inside.

No updates.
Not from doctors. Not from nurses.
Not even from God.

In that corridor time stopped pretending it was linear.
I did not know whether to pray for a miracle or prepare for a funeral.
Every breath felt provisional.

That grey zone is where you stop being religious and become real.
Where no mantra survives intact.
Where no theory keeps you warm.
Where no guru can hand you a promise without lying.

Only silence..Only waiting..
Only the kind of patience that tears your soul open from the inside and asks what remains when hope is stripped of outcomes.

There was a grey zone that arrived more quietly.

Someone who mattered beyond measure.
No name for it..No category that fit.
No status that made it respectable.

Just a deep soulful connection that healed me and unsettled me at the same time.

I did not know whether to call it divine or delusional.
Whether it was meant to awaken something and leave.
What it taught me did not arrive as comfort.

Some soul contracts are not meant to be completed.
They are meant to be honoured.

Some people enter your life like poems
and leave like riddles you do not solve but carry.

We are trained to crave answers.
Figure it out..Fix it..Name it.

Make it make sense.
But life is not a courtroom.
It does not respond to cross-examination.

Life is a dance.
And the grey zones are the pauses in the music.
The breath between steps.
The moment when you realise movement does not always mean progress.

The more you try to define what is undefined the more it slips away.
And maybe that is not failure...Maybe that is precision.

The grey zone taught me to stop begging for endings.
To stop needing pain to justify itself.
To stop demanding that love arrive in approved forms.

It taught me that not every story has a villain.
Not every heartbreak is a mistake.
Not every silence is empty.

Some silences are sacred.

I learned that some answers never arrive in words.
They arrive as a quiet settling in the body.
A knowing that does not announce itself.

The Divine does not always respond with signs or sounds.
Sometimes silence is the guidance.

I also learned to stop needing everything to make sense.
Some answers arrive years later.
Some arrive only after you have grown enough not to misuse them.
Some never arrive at all.

And somehow I learned to live with that.

Not by tolerating it.
By listening.

So I chose to sit in the unknown.
To breathe without conclusion.
To love without a name.
To heal without full understanding.
To walk without a map.

In that surrender I met a version of myself who did not need certainty to be whole.
A self that did not demand a plot twist to feel validated.
A self that did not confuse chaos with punishment.

A self that could finally say
I may not know what this is but I know it is sacred.

I remember another moment of grey.

A job offer on one end of the phone.
A child needing me on the other.

One promised validation.
The other promised belonging.

I stood in the kitchen holding both like two broken wings.
Neither whole..Neither wrong.

The decision was not clear.
The consequences were real.

I chose my family.
And for years I doubted it.

No applause followed.
No trophy arrived.
Only whispers that I had given up too soon and long nights wondering if I had failed.

Years later my child now grown said quietly
Thank you for being there when I did not know how to ask for it.

Clarity did not arrive through logic or proof.
It arrived through time.
Through love.

That is the kind of clarity the grey gives.
Delayed.. Disguised.. Divine.

The rarest grey is not the blur itself.
It is the moment inside the blur when you decide to trust your becoming without witnesses.

When you stop searching for light at the end of the tunnel because you realise you have become the light learning how to walk through it.

G³ Goonj~

The grey zone is not a waiting room.
It is a womb.
It does not pause your life.
It prepares your soul.
It teaches you to bloom while the fog is still thick.
To rise without needing to be clearly seen.
To love without knowing what comes next.
To live not because you have figured it out
but because you have finally stopped trying to control it.

Once you survive the grey zone the world no longer owns you.

Timelines lose their authority.
Answers lose their leverage.
Other people's understanding stops being a prerequisite for your peace.

You move with a quiet power.

The kind that does not explain itself.
The kind that knows when to stay when to walk and when to simply watch life unfold.

Your prayers change.
They stop asking for rescue and start asking for remembrance.
You stop chasing healing and begin embodying it.

You realise you are no longer waiting for clarity to begin living.
You are living as clarity.

Unwritten grey zones, begins to make sense that not every pressure is meant to be endured.
Sometimes you are pressed against a wall…not because you are meant to break it, not because you are meant to survive suffocation but it was never a door to begin with.
What feels like resistance is often redirection. The moment isn't asking you to prove strength or loyalty; it is asking for discernment. To pause.. To turn.. Or to step back before harm masquerades as destiny.

The grey zone do not weaken you.
It refined you.
Stripped you to soul.
Teaches you to walk without the crutches of certainty.

And it leaves you with the rarest grace of all.
The ability to bloom even in the blur.

I am no longer afraid of chapters that remain unfinished.
I trust pages that stay blank longer than expected.
I trust pauses that feel like mistakes while they are forming truth.

If this chapter resonates with you..good.
That means its alive.

Some stories do not end..They mature.
And this one is still becoming me.

CHAPTER 32

SHOWDOWN WITH THE INVISIBLE THREAD

~A LULLABY. A LOSS. A LEGACY.

"A tribute I live with every day"
A gratitude etched into my nervous system.

Her presence did not end with her death.
It did not become a memory you visit occasionally.
It became something ongoing.

A requiem written in recipes.
A resurrection that lives in memory.

This is for every daughter still instinctively dialing "Maa."

The older I get, the more I realise I never really moved out of my mother's heart.
I changed cities. Changed my surname.
I became a wife. A mother. A woman others lean on.
Yet I remained her little girl.
Tucked into her ribcage like a song she never finished humming.

She was always my first number.
First ring. First instinct.

A kids fever.
A cracked pressure cooker lid.
A fear I could not name.

"Mamma."

That one word carried everything.
My SOS.. My compass.. My invisible thread..

Now the line is quiet.
And I don't know who to call for the kind of ache that only silence amplifies.

The Soup That Saved Me

I remember the hour.
I had cried myself hoarse. My child would not stop vomiting.
My husband was out of town.

I stood by the kitchen sink hollow and hungry.
For food. For reassurance. For someone older than me.

I called her.

"Mummy kya banaun. Woh kuch nahin kha rahi. I don't know what to do. What to cook..she's not eating anything"

She replied without panic. Without drama.
In that voice that had stitched me together more times than I can count.

"Halke haath se moong daal ki khichdi bana.
Thoda jeera. Thoda haldi.
Aur pyaar daal dena."

Make lentil and rice soup with soft hands so the grains remain soft and unbroken..then feed her with love.

I followed her words like scripture.
she ate.. Quietly.. Peacefully.

I broke.

Because what filled that bowl was not just khichdi.

It was her hands. Her knowing. Her steadiness.
Crossing cities and Crossing phone lines.
Arriving intact into the chaos of my motherhood.

Even today I cannot cook that dish without weeping.

She was my Everything Hotline ..!
Everything ran through her.

How to drape a saree.
How to soften an apology.
Which bhog to prepare for Navratri.
How to lift stubborn ghee stains from brass diyas.

And when she did not have the answer it arrived wrapped in laughter.. she'd say..you're a grown women now..figure it out yourself..

Echo of her laughter carried the sound of saris drying in the sun…Of stories she never formally told.
Even her scoldings were seasoned.
Like the extra tadka she added when the dal felt unsure of itself.
She'd always sway away from the subject enlightening much more than I could remember..

Was it too much to need her this often.
Was I dependent or devoted ..?

Even after marriage..Even after children.
Even after growing into the version of woman the world calls independent.

I still went back to her.
For validation..For remedies..For recipes..For random rants.
Sometimes just to hear her breathe and be around her..

Often, hung up without saying much.
Knowing she was there and it was enough.

Now the silence has a sound…It howls..!

When her First Home Began Packing..
Toward the end her voice slowed.
Her memory skipped..Her hands hesitated.
A bit later speech lost..
It was as if her body had already begun folding itself away.

But she never told me she was leaving.
Mothers do not do that.
They do not frighten their children with goodbyes.

And then the thread frayed.

No warning..No farewell speech..Just gone.

What I observed from her life..
My mother never stopped to sit for herself.

She cooked while her joints ached.
Fed neighbour's before herself.
Held space for everyone while hiding her own fatigue.

She believed love meant sacrifice.

What I now understand is this.
Unbalanced giving is not virtue..It is erosion.

If you are young and able.. give freely.
If you are aging or fragile.. protect your waters.

You cannot nourish others from a cracked vessel.
This is what her leaving taught me.
This is what I now whisper to women I meet.

The Recipes Are Mine Now
She hardly ever wrote them down.

They lived in her gestures.
In the clink of her karwachauth bangles while stirring
ma ki dal (dal makhni)
In pauses before adding salt.
In accuracy without measurement.
Her hands deep in the dish tasting..checking..adding love..
I loved her passion for food..

Now I recreate them..Each time something inside me trembles. Her Kashmiri palak paneer, chicken Hawaiian salad, her baked mutton, besan wali louki..sweet mango murabba, her pizzas.

She loved South Indian dishes as much as she liked North Indian food.. but Sambar was her favourite with extra drumsticks..
And just like that..cooking was no longer domestic for me.
It's devotional..It's memory work..It's communion.. its her passion. And each recipe a way to summon her, from wherever love goes when it leaves the body.

My Invisible Thread..
People speak of grief like a phase.
Something to cross and exit.
I know better.

Grief is a second skin.
It stays..and while it softens..
It teaches you how to listen differently.
She still parents me.
Through instinct..Through restraint.
Through the nudge to rest..Through an inexplicable craving for tamarind, aloo bukara or prunes at 2 a.m.

She is the air that moves the curtain when I whisper Maa..

My Showdown

My showdown was not with her leaving.
It was with what her leaving exposed.

I had built my inner safety on her availability.
On her voice answering before the second ring.
On the certainty that no matter how old I became
someone older than me still existed.

When that vanished..
I stood inside a silence I had never rehearsed.
There was no one to call..
No higher authority to pass the decision to.
No maternal witness to my panic.
Yes my dad and brother..but not an equation a daughter has with her mother..that void cant be filled.

Grief was not the hardest part.
Responsibility was.

For the first time I had to become the place of reassurance instead of seeking it.
I had to answer my own emergencies.
Calm my own storms..Hold myself the way she once held me.

That was the rupture..Not loss, but inheritance arriving without consent.
And not to forgot she trained us all well since she was
Bed-ridden.. very slowly, with time.. we demanded less of her.

G³ Goonj~

She left..Just like that.
An integral part of my existence paused.

Here is what grief teaches if you let it.
They do not disappear..They reorganise.

They breathe through you..They rise in your rituals..
They become the recipe of your soul.

Now I hold the thread..

One day my daughter will dial me.
And I will answer with what was once given to me.
Food.. Comfort.. Steadiness..

Today I am her refuge..Her thread..till I'm visible.

I'm the one now who holds her..where she once guided, protected and anchored..
I'm the living connection that keeps her held to life, meaning and belonging.

Some bonds do not break when bodies leave.
They relocate..

A mother does not disappear..she decentralises.
Her voice dissolves into instinct.
Her touch converts into muscle memory.
Her protection rewires itself as intuition.

What once came from outside now rises from within.
This is not absence..This is internalisation.

And this is how lineage survives.
Not as nostalgia but as embodied knowing.

Not just this chapter, this book is yours Maa..

May your name rise in every flame I light.
May your care restore every soul I heal.
May your memory nourish every meal I make.
May your love be the greatest inheritance, I carry,
never stops feeding me.

Minna Pahwa
05-01-1949 to 18-06-2025

Believing her presence moves with grace, guiding, watching, holding me beyond sight.

In loving memory of my gorgeous Maa..

CHAPTER 33

SHOWDOWN WITH THE WHISPERS OF DISBELIEFS

~DISBELIEF A NECESSARY CROSSING

G³ Goonj~

This chapter is not about doubt.

It is about initiation through erosion.

Most spiritual narratives rely on spectacle. Loud crises. Visible collapse. Sudden awakening. This chapter refuses that grammar. What unfolds here is far more dangerous. A phase where nothing appears broken yet something essential is thinning out quietly steadily almost politely.

The Whisper is not an antagonist.
It is a threshold intelligence.
It arrives only when the psyche is strong enough to begin separating inherited fear from lived truth. That is why it enters early. Childhood is the moment consciousness first learns how to turn against itself. The classroom is not about performance. It is the instant identity becomes self-observing. Innocence fractures not into shame but into evaluation.

From that moment the chapter traces something rare. Disbelief does not destroy the self. It postpones embodiment.
You remain functional. Accomplished. Devotional. Relational.

But not fully inhabited.

That is the ache the observer registers. Not weakness. Dimming. A presence that has stepped slightly outside its own body.

What gives this chapter its gravity is that disbelief is never conquered. There is no affirmation arc. No victory language. No transcendence fantasy. The Whisper dissolves only when it is no longer required.

Which reveals the deeper truth..Disbelief is temporary scaffolding. It exists until trust moves from concept into tissue.

It appears when belief is still mental.
It leaves when trust becomes somatic.

That shift is the true ending of Volume One.

Volume One was never about healing. It was about becoming capable of holding truth without distortion. Of surviving clarity. Of staying present when illusion collapses. Only then does the nervous system become strong enough to receive responsibility instead of relief.

So the silence at the end of this chapter is not peace.
It is readiness.

Volume One ends when the seeker stops asking why.
Volume Two begins when life starts asking how.

That is the command that was missing earlier.
Not power over the Whisper.
Authority over presence.

Disbelief does not leave in spectacle.
It leaves when consciousness grows up.
Because belief only prepares you to kneel.
What comes next demands that you stand.

And there is no strength left. No stored courage. Not even the illusion of readiness.

Yet the world has already placed its weight on your shoulders.
Expectation does not wait for recovery.
Service does not ask if you are healed enough.

This is where belief ends.

And something far more unforgiving begins.
Once disbelief loosens its grip you are no longer protected by confusion as Clarity demands consequence.

FROM THE VANTAGE...

From survival to elevation, you have walked with me through every fracture and every remembering.
You have felt the truth echo from my soul across these pages.

And as I look back now, I see this clearly..
The Showdown was never with the world. It was always with myself.

With the fearful child who lay awake in the shadows of early upbringing, learning silence before words..before..obedience.. before courage.

That fear followed me into my teenage years, whispering that love must be earned, that approval must be begged, that belonging was fragile.

As I stepped into adulthood, the fear changed costumes. It became the fear of not being loved, the ache of pouring oceans into people who could not even hold a cup. I mistook validation for devotion and in the process, I drowned in my own waters.

Motherhood arrived like earth.. rooting me, grounding me, forcing me to give life even when I felt lifeless. It was there that I first tasted unconditional love, along with the exhaustion of carrying worlds on my shoulders that longed for rest.
My fire was still dim, my air still restless, my water still flooding, yet the soil of motherhood gave me a place to stand.

Then came the breaking and the awakening.
The Showdowns with shame, despair, fragile masculinity, toxic dynamics, desire, love, judgment, unbearable grief...with the

monsters inside and the gods above. Every chapter was not a war I fought..
it was a mirror I faced.

Through each crack, each collapse, each surrender, I began to see the hidden architect beneath it all...The perfect play of Elements.

Air had given me.. imagination and chaos.
Water had given me.. compassion as well as drowning.
Earth had given me grounding and stagnation.
Fire had been missing.. the courage, the will, the roar..
until I chose to light it myself.

And then there was **Ether.**
Not something I cultivated, earned or controlled.
It was the quiet intelligence that held all the elements together.
The space in which my fear could be seen without being obeyed.
The stillness where I was no longer trying to fix myself.

The place where something larger than me had always been holding the centre... it was the presence I felt, when effort stopped.
The unseen order beneath every collapse and every becoming.
The place where God did not speak but was unmistakably there.

It was within this space where Spirituality entered my life..not as an escape but as alchemy.
Through balance, I learned that the elements within me were not enemies but teachers. They shaped the girl who hid, the woman who searched, the mother who gave and the seeker who surrendered.

They shaped me from where I began trembling to where I stand now...steady.

And where will I be..?
Wherever the elements align..

Because now know, fear may start the journey but balance completes it.

"The Showdown was never about fighting my life.
It was about remembering that,
I am air...I am water...I am fire...I am earth...I am ether..
And when they bow to each other inside me,
life itself bows in return."

G³ Goonj~

Something settled after that remembering.
And for the first time, I was not chasing healing, fixing or meaning.
I was simply present inside myself.

The noise softened.
The inner elements found their rhythm.
What once felt fractured now felt aligned.

I did not feel finished but I felt whole.
And in that wholeness, I rested.

This was the end of my survival.
This was the beginning of balance.

Volume One ends here.
At the point where seeking exhausts itself.
Where the mind fractures just enough to stop pretending it is in control.

Somewhere between exhaustion and its own clever manipulations,
I thought the storm was over.
I didn't know the trial..the real trial..had not even begun.

What follows is not comfort.

It is maturity..!

Service without glamour.
Healing without applause.
Spiritual intelligence tested not in isolation but
in Relationship..in Power..in Conflict..in fatigue..
in quiet, uncelebrated endurance.

Volume Two does not arrive as continuation.
It arrives as reckoning.

It begins after belief has completed its function and can no longer shield you.
After doubt has thinned and clarity has sharpened into demand.
This is not the story of becoming spiritual.
This is the story of what spirituality costs once it starts moving through you.
When healing turns operational.
When service becomes unavoidable.
When silence is replaced by responsibility and knowing is tested in real time through people consequence and consequence again.

Volume One has prepared the ground.
Volume Two exposes what grows there.

As not everything can survive the light.

This was the fracture.
The call...The edge..

And the silence that follows is not absence.

It is initiation..!

I step onto higher ground.
I pause for a final glance..not with grief, not with longing,
only with recognition of the terrain that shaped my sight.
From here, destruction makes sense..So does the light..

The path ahead is carved, not destined.
Without explanation, I move...
What lies ahead is sharper for those expecting quiet.
There are still showdowns waiting, not to test endurance,
but to fracture perception and dismantle false clarity.
They force open doors in the mind that cannot be entered gently.
The door first encountered still stands.. What waited behind it will be named.
This is not where the story settles...This is where it tightens.